Skills for Success for your fourth grader

A+ Student

Written by
Barbara Adams

Illustrations by
Kelly McMahon

Cover Photography by Anthony Nex of Anthony Nex Photography

Photo Credits: © 1997 Comstock, Inc.: 3, 8, 13, 17, 19, 22, 25, 26, 30, 36, 39, 45, 48, 50, 53, 56, 57, 58, 59, 60, 65, 66, 68

FS-23005 Skills for Success for Your Fourth Grader
All rights reserved—Printed in the U. S. A. Copyright © 1997 Frank Schaffer Publications, Inc.

Table of Contents

The Fabulous Fourth Grader!

Parents wear many hats every day. Each one is equally important, but sometimes parents are nervous about wearing the hat of "teacher" for their child. The truth is that all day every day the invisible "teacher hat" is perched on your head, perhaps even on top of another hat you may be wearing at the moment! The joy of parenting comes with making the most of every opportunity to be your child's "teacher."

Parents can be nervous about performing the role of teacher because they are not sure what expectations or goals are realistic for their child at each level. This book is aimed at helping you understand, appreciate, and accentuate the learning that your child is ready to experience.

You were and still are your child's first and most important teacher. By becoming familiar with the skills a fourth grader needs, you can be more efficient and effective as you continue in that role.

Fourth graders have fabulous abilities and aspirations. There are no limits to what they can achieve as they embark upon the intermediate grades.

* They are **spirited** individuals with an enthusiasm for life and learning.

* They are **cooperative**. They know some things can only be accomplished through teamwork.

* They are **dramatic**. They feel emotions deeply and do not hide them.

* They are **dedicated** to their ideas, projects, friends, and family.

* They are **proud** of their accomplishments and want to succeed.

* They are **compassionate** to those in need.

* They are **innovative**. They can put ideas or items together to make new and wonderful things.

* They are **perceptive** to details and changes in their surroundings.

* They are **delightful** and will amaze you with both their innocence and sophistication.

* They are **ready to learn and grow** with your direction and the ideas in this book.

The Keys to Using This Book

Be a Learner

Be ready to tell your child that you don't know something. A question from your child indicates interest in the topic, but you don't need to feel embarrassed if you don't know the answer. The important step is to help your child look for an answer.

Teach to the Moment

Remember that the best time to teach anything is the moment your child has expressed curiosity about it. If your child asks a question about the phases of the moon, try to provide information, look it up with him or her in a science book or encyclopedia, and watch the sky. If you have access to the Internet or a computer with a multimedia reference tool, use that to gain instant facts to share.

Teach Academic Skills

The first section of this book provides a guide for you that's full of activities that center around the topics fourth graders study in school. Use it to help your child better understand a topic that is being taught and to enhance the learning your child is doing at school. Use the background information and the ideas to provide enjoyable interaction with your child.

Teach Social Skills

The next section centers around social skills. Even the most intelligent child will be less successful in school without good personal skills. These interpersonal skills are critical for positive relationships to develop and for your child to feel worthwhile. Use this section to provide an approach to a problem or an opening to discuss a topic. With prior discussion about these vital skills, your child will have strategies to deal with concerns when they appear.

Promote Home and School Cooperation

The next section of the book gives you practical ideas for how to navigate home and school interaction on a daily basis. There are suggestions for organizing, communicating with the educational community, conferencing with teachers, and getting involved at school.

Give Praise

Included in the book are reward items. Use these to show your child that you are proud of his or her efforts. Children respond to positive reinforcement. Teachers know that the more specific the praise, the better. "Good job!" is great to hear, but more repeat performances come from phrases such as "You wrote that story so neatly that it is easy for me to read. That shows me you are proud of it, too!"

Give Practice

The final section is skill pages for your child that reinforce the activities suggested in the first section. Use them to check on your child's understanding of the skill. Use them to provide individual practice for a skill. Use them to provide a chance for your child to demonstrate progress! If your child has difficulty, you may want to repeat an activity or choose a new approach to helping him or her master that skill.

Reading for Fourth Graders

Reading is a basic tool of learning and a necessary skill in everyday living. Almost every school subject—math, science, spelling, social studies, health, art, and music—depends on your child's ability to read. There are a multitude of skills that your child must learn and apply to be an effective reader and learner. The activities in this book reinforce the following skill areas:

COMPREHENSION

* drawing conclusions
* understanding a series of steps in a process
* classifying
* sequencing
* interpreting symbols
* identifying main idea and details
* identifying similarities and differences
* identifying main events in a story

LITERATURE

* analyzing literary elements— character, plot, setting
* recognizing author's language and style, such as using onomatopoeic words
* literary devices—definition, summary, simile, antonym, appositive
* genres—folklore, fable, myth, biography, poetry

STUDY SKILLS

* organizing information
* using the card catalog or a computer catalog search tool
* using the Dewey Decimal System
* using reference sources
* following oral and written directions
* using parts of a book to find information—table of contents, index, glossary
* using graphics to interpret text
* reading a newspaper

VOCABULARY AND DECODING

* recognizing word categories
* understanding analogies
* using structural analysis—prefixes and suffixes
* recognizing compound words
* using context clues

ORAL READING

* reading with fluency and clarity
* using expression

FAMILY READING FUN

Tell Me a Story

Invite your child to help you look through his or her bookshelves for examples of folktales, fairy tales, fables, tall tales, hero tales, and myths. When you find two different forms, such as a fable and a tall tale, read them aloud together. Then talk about the characteristics that are unique, as well as similar, to each form. For example, a fable is a short tale that teaches a moral or lesson, usually through the use of animal characters that talk and act like humans. A tall tale is filled with exaggerations about a larger-than-life hero who is the biggest, strongest, or bravest, and who tackles and solves any problem that comes along. After reading several stories, work together to create one of your own to tell the family or that involves people in your family.

Picture This

It is said that a picture is worth a thousand words. Ask your child what he or she thinks this means. Encourage your child to explain how pictures, photographs, and illustrations are particularly helpful when reading about people and events at different times in history or in unfamiliar places. In contrast, have your child look for two fictional books or stories, one with pictures and one without. Together, read a chapter or descriptive paragraph from each. Talk about how the accompanying artwork can sometimes help a reader to better understand a character, the setting, or an event. Then ask your child if he or she would rather read a story with illustrations that interpret the text or one without and use his or her own imagination.

Just for fun as you read aloud a description from a book or story, have your child and another family member each illustrate the character, event, or setting. Then have the two illustrators compare and discuss their interpretations.

Reading Aloud

If you have a tape recorder, have your child practice his or her oral reading skills by reading aloud from different kinds of printed materials including picture books, chapter books, textbooks, newspapers, and magazines. Play back the tape after each session and encourage your child to listen with a critical ear for fluency, clarity, expressiveness, and so on. When your child becomes comfortable with hearing his or her voice, suggest that he or she choose a favorite children's story to record for a younger child.

A Family Reading Circle

Visit the library or the bookstore and encourage your child to select a new book to read. (See the next page for suggested titles. Your child's teacher may also have some suggestions.) Then invite your child to read aloud to you and other family members for 10 to 15 minutes each night. You may want to take turns reading. Discuss the story as you go. Encourage family members to think about what might happen next, how they feel about certain characters, why they think a character is behaving in a certain way, and so on.

GREAT BOOKS FOR FOURTH GRADERS

Here are some titles you may want to look for at the library or bookstore.

Folklore, Fables, and Myths

And It Is Still That Way by Byrd Baylor (Trails West, 1988)

Fables by Arnold Lobel (Harper & Row, 1980)

Peace Tales: World Folktales to Talk About by Margaret Read MacDonald (Linnet, 1992)

The People Could Fly: American Black Folktales by Virginia Hamilton (Knopf, 1985)

Chapter Books

Anastasia Krupnik by Lois Lowry (Houghton Mifflin, 1979)

Bunnicula by Deborah and James Howe (Atheneum, 1979)

Help! I'm a Prisoner in the Library by Eth Clifford (Houghton Mifflin, 1979)

The Indian in the Cupboard by Lynne Reid Banks (Doubleday, 1981)

James and the Giant Peach by Roald Dahl (Knopf, 1961)

The Secret of the Seal by Deborah Davis (Crown, 1989)

The Skirt by Gary Soto (Delacorte Press, 1992)

The Stories Julian Tells by Ann Cameron (Pantheon, 1981)

Tales of a Fourth Grade Nothing by Judy Blume (Dutton, 1972)

Thank You, Jackie Robinson by Barbara Cohen (Lothrop, 1974)

Three Terrible Trins by Dick King-Smith (Crown, 1994)

The Trumpet of the Swans by E.B. White (Harper & Row, 1970)

Yang the Youngest and His Terrible Ear by Lesley Namioka (Joy Street, 1992)

Poetry

Falling Up by Shel Silverstein (HarperCollins, 1996)

Nathaniel Talking by Eloise Greenfield (Writers and Readers, 1988)

The Oxford Book of Poetry compiled by Edward Blishen (reissued by Bedrick, 1984)

Small Poems by Valerie Worth (Farrar, Straus & Giroux, 1972)

Informational Books

The Animal Atlas by Barbara Taylor (Knopf, 1992)

Bard of Avon: The Story of William Shakespeare by Diane Stanley and Peter Vennema (Morrow, 1992)

A Boy Called Slow: The True Story of Sitting Bull by Joseph Bruchac (Philomel, 1994)

Glow in the Dark Constellations by C.E. Thompson (Brookehouse, 1989)

If You Traveled on the Underground Railroad by Ellen Levine (Scholastic, 1993)

Richard Orr's Nature Cross-Sections by Moira Butterfield (Dorling Kindersley, 1995)

Starry Messenger: Galileo Galilei by Peter Sís (Frances Foster, 1996)

LIBRARY SMARTS

A library is a wonderful resource for books, magazines, CDs and cassettes, videos, and other items. Teach your child how to get around the library and how to ask for help. Encourage your child to check out materials using his or her own library card.

Organization

Libraries often have both a children's section and an adult section divided into fiction, nonfiction, and reference areas. Usually reference materials may not be checked out. In addition, there may be a Young Adult section with themes and reading levels geared for middle school and high school students.

Card Catalog

Most libraries have switched or are switching to a computerized catalog. If you are unfamiliar with how to use your library's computer system, be sure to ask a librarian for help. Your child should learn how to conduct a computer search for an item by title, author, or subject. When doing a computer search by subject, teach your child to be fairly specific and to give additional words that help focus the search. For example, if your child is looking for a book on kangaroos for a report, a search on "animals" might yield over 1000 titles. A search on "kangaroos juvenile nonfiction" might yield 10 titles within the children's section.

Call Numbers

A book's call number lets you know where to find it in the library. Teach your child that fiction is arranged in alphabetical order by the author's last name. Most K–12 school libraries and public libraries organize nonfiction books using the Dewey Decimal System.

398.22
King Arthur

You can cut out a copy of this handy bookmark guide for your child to take to the library when searching for nonfiction materials.

Where to Look

Dewey Decimal Categories

000—099	**General Works** (encyclopedias)
100—199	**Philosophy**
200—299	**Religion**
300—399	**Social Sciences** (holidays, folklore)
400—499	**Language** (dictionaries, foreign language books)
500—599	**Pure Sciences** (math, animals)
600—699	**Applied Science** (medicine, engineering, homemaking)
700—799	**Arts** (art, music, sports)
800—899	**Literature** (poetry, plays)
900—999	**Geography** and **History**

 FS-23005 Skills for Success for Your Fourth Grader • © Frank Schaffer Publications, Inc.

LITERARY ACTIVITIES

What's the Plot?

Take some time to read a short story or book with your child. Afterward, ask your child to identify as many of the main events as he or she can recall. Jot down each one as a statement on a separate index card or slip of paper. You may want to suggest some as well. Then scramble the cards. Challenge your child to rearrange them in the correct sequence.

How Does It End?

Look for a short story in a children's magazine that you think your child would enjoy and which he or she has not yet read. Cover or cut out the ending. Have your child read the beginning and middle and tell how he or she thinks the story will end. Then have your child read the ending and compare it to his or her own.

How Clever!

Remind your child that authors sometimes give clues to help their readers know the meaning of important words and ideas in sentences. Share these examples of literary devices:

The sepal is one of the leaflike parts which makes up the outer covering of a flower. (definition)

Everyone says Jake is uncouth. His bad language, harsh voice, and terrible manners seem to show they are right. (summary)

Meg's eyes glistened like bright stars twinkling in the night sky. (simile)

Milt is always anxious about something. We can't use the word calm to describe him! (antonym)

The thesaurus, a book of synonyms, is a great help when you don't want to use the same words over and over again. (appositive)

Together read a page from a textbook, a novel, or an article in a magazine or newspaper to look for more examples of these techniques. Encourage your child to look for such clues whenever he or she is reading and comes across an unfamiliar word.

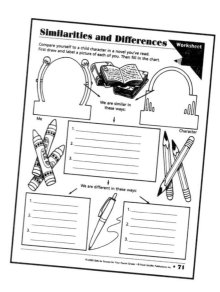

Similarities and Differences

Determining how things are alike and different is an important reading comprehension skill. Your child can compare himself or herself to a favorite child character from a novel. If your child isn't sure what to compare, suggest age, sex, physical and behavioral traits, likes and dislikes, and so on. Your child can use page 71 to record the comparisons. Extend the activity to other curriculum areas as well, using your child's textbooks as reference sources. For example, have your child read about and then compare and contrast multiplication and division, classical music and rock music, football and soccer, and so on.

KITCHEN READING ACTIVITIES

Clipping Coupons

Do you save supermarket coupons? If you do, ask your child to help out. It provides a great opportunity to practice reading and classifying skills. When you have gathered a pile of coupon pages, give your child a list of products to look for and clip out. Then have your child organize the coupons into groups, such as breads, canned foods, beauty products, and so on. If you have a coupon organizer, let your child file them. The next time you go shopping, ask your child to retrieve the coupons for the specific products you want to purchase.

Do You Believe It?

Have your child gather a variety of magazine ads for brand-name foods and clothing, restaurants, toys and games, tobacco, alcoholic beverages, and so on. Point out that advertisements are paid for by the producers who want to convince consumers to buy products, even products that are known to be harmful to one's health. Encourage your child to study each ad and describe how the advertiser tries to persuade potential consumers and customers. Then ask your child if he or she believes the ad and to explain why or why not.

How Do You Make Pancakes?

The next time you plan to make pancakes, bake a batch of cookies from scratch, make a pot of chicken soup, or prepare a dish that requires reading a recipe, invite your child to help. Begin by having your child read the recipe. Then see how much he or she recalls by asking questions such as the following: *What ingredients do we need? What utensils do we need? Does the oven have to be preheated? At what temperature? How long will it take to bake (simmer, cook)? What do we do first? second? third? and so on.* Have your child then check the recipe for accuracy.

Just for fun, try this activity. Choose five or six recipes for your child's favorite dishes and desserts. For each recipe you

will need three index cards, one to record the name of the dish or dessert, one to record the ingredients, and one to record the steps. Mix up the cards. Then challenge your child to correctly match up the name, ingredients, and directions for each.

How Much Should I Take?

Gather some of the medications that your child takes for colds, fevers, upset stomachs, and so on. Talk about the importance of taking the proper dosages. Then help your child locate and read the information on the labels, packaging, and inserts that indicates how much your child should take, how often, possible side effects, the date of expiration, and possible contraindications for taking each medication.

MORE READING ACTIVITIES

What's On at 8 O'Clock?

Give your child practice using a newspaper or magazine television guide. Challenge your child to answer questions like these: *What programs are on at 8:00 P.M. tonight? Which shows end at 8:30? How many stations broadcast the news at 5:00 P.M.? 6:00 P.M.? What cable television movie do you think everyone in the family would enjoy watching this week? What time does it begin and end? Will it repeat at other times?*

Textbook Talk

When your child brings home textbooks, take a few minutes to see how well he or she understands their specific features, such as the table of contents, index, glossary, and chapter and unit reviews. Thumb through the books together to discover the features. Then ask questions such as the following: *Would you look in the index, the glossary, or the table of contents to find out what a word means? Where would you look to see if your science book has a chapter on energy? What is the focus of the first unit of the social studies book? Does it contain a unit review?*

How Supportive!

Fourth graders are often required to read informational books and reference materials in order to write a report. Being able to skim paragraphs for the main idea is a valuable skill that will help them recognize if the information is needed or not. You can give your child practice identifying details that support a main idea. Copy the sentences of a paragraph from one of your child's textbooks on individual strips of paper. Mix them up. Challenge your child to identify the main idea sentence and the detail sentences, and then to arrange the sentences in order.

Symbolically Speaking

Talk about how information is often communicated without words, but with symbols instead. Together look for symbols on the packaging and containers of the products you and your family use, such as bleach, furniture polish, and shampoo. Talk about what the symbols mean. The next time you are out with your child, look for signs that indicate locations, warn of hazards and dangers, or give commands such as "No smoking." You can use page 72 to reinforce the activity.

Dots and Letters

Can your child identify the system of reading used by the blind in which a person runs one's fingertips over a series of raised dots? The system is called Braille after Louis Braille who invented it when he was only 15 years old. Have your child see page 73 for an example of the Braille alphabet and an activity.

READING THE NEWSPAPER

The newspaper is a timely, informative, entertaining, and inexpensive reading resource.

What's In a Newspaper?

A newspaper has something for everyone. Do a quick search through the newspaper with your child. As you look at headlines, photographs, and the items listed below, call out whether they are of interest to kids, teenagers, adults, or all ages. Can you find these items?

* weather forecast
* comics
* sports standings
* movie or TV listings
* advice columns
* letters to the editor
* classified ads—Lost and Found, instruments for sale, free kittens

Then help your child understand how your newspaper is organized. Note whether sections and pages are lettered or numbered or both. Are sections organized by topic—world and national news, local news, sports, business, entertainment? Locate the index and study it to see which items it lists.

How Comical!

Gather some comic strips from the newspaper, including a few episodes from the same strip. Invite your child to read aloud the strips to you and then answer some questions that require identifying cause and effect, drawing conclusions, making judgments, thinking creatively, and so on. For example, encourage your child to suggest why something happened, what your child would have said or done in a similar situation, or what age or type of audience the strip was designed for.

Skimming Headlines

Headlines summarize an article or story and catch the reader's interest. With your child, skim through the headlines of the day's newspaper. Then ask your child questions such as these: *Which headlines sound interesting? Which stories do you think might involve children? Which headlines involve humor or a play on words?*

The 5 W's

A news story usually answers the 5 W's—who, what, where, when, and why—in the first, or lead, paragraph. Let your child choose an article. Have your child read it to find out the 5 W's and other interesting details. Encourage your child to talk about it over dinner with other members of the family. You may want to use page 74 of this book for further practice.

Sports Standings

Show your child how to read the standings for a current sport. Explain how the leading teams are listed first and which columns show wins, losses, games back, or other information. Then play a find-and-answer riddle game. Take turns asking riddles such as this one: *This team is in the Central Division. It has 20 wins and 5 losses. It is tied with Detroit. Who is it?*

VOCABULARY

Before and After

When reading, your child will undoubtedly encounter unfamiliar words. Point out that recognizing and knowing the meanings of prefixes or suffixes can help a reader decipher new words. Look in newspapers or magazines for words containing prefixes and suffixes and circle them. Together analyze each word by breaking it into its parts, noting the meaning of the prefix or suffix and the meaning of the word to which it was added. For example, in the word *unfriendly,* the prefix *un* means "not" and the suffix *ly* means "in the manner," so *unfriendly* means "not in the manner of a friend." Extend the activity by having your child build new words by adding prefixes and suffixes to words such as these: cycle, inform, usual, act, govern, sense, write, thought, real, like, beauty.

Your child can cut out a copy of the box below to keep as a handy reference at his or her workspace.

Compound Interest

Write the following words on separate index cards or strips of paper: *forehead, floodlight, background, barefoot, fingertip, flagship, toenail, salesman, powerhouse, soapstone, handball, underbrush, toothache, backyard.* As your child reads the words, see if he or she recognizes that they are all compound words, formed from two separate words. If any of the words are unfamiliar, encourage your child to think about the meanings of the two words that form each compound. Have a dictionary handy to check. Then cut apart each compound word into two words, scramble the word parts, and challenge your child to use them to make new words. Here are some possible combinations: *forefinger, football, toothbrush, handsoap, shipyard, underground, headache, flagstone, foreman, houselight, bareback.*

Prefixes		Suffixes			
anti-	(against)	-able	(capable of being)	-ist	(one who does)
bi-	(two)	-ance	(state of being)	-ity	(state of)
com-	(with)	-ation	(state of)	-ive	(tendency toward)
de-	(from)	-en	(made of)	-less	(without)
dis-	(not, apart)	-ence	(state or quality of)	-ly	(similar in manner or appearance)
em-, en-	(in)	-er	(one who does)		
ex-	(out, from)	-eous	(like, full of)	-ment	(state of, result of)
im-	(not, into)	-ful	(full of)	-ness	(quality, state of being)
in-	(not)	-ian	(one who does)		
inter-	(between)	-ible	(capable of being)	-our	(full of)
mis-	(wrong)	-ic	(like, made of)	-ty	(quality of)
non-	(not)	-ion	(condition, quality)	-ure	(denoting action)
ob-, op-	(against)	-ious	(like, full of)	-ward	(in direction of)
pre-	(before)	-ish	(like)	-y	(like, state or quality of)
pro-	(in front of)				
re-	(again)				
tri-	(three)				
un-	(not, opposite of)				

MORE VOCABULARY ACTIVITIES

The Sounds of Things

Read aloud the following words with expression: *slurp, twang, zip, ding dong, buzz, hiss.* Discuss how each one sounds like the action or object it represents. Ask your child to identify what makes each sound. Then challenge your child to name other "onomatopoeic" words. Here are a few: *beep, bong, chirp, clink, flippity flop, grind, honk, moo, murmur, ping, quack, slurp, thump.* Have your child look for poems with onomatopoeic words, such as "Clock" by Valerie Worth and "Bees" by Jack Prelutsky. Encourage your child to create his or her own poems using onomatopoeic words.

Be Sensible!

For fun give your child the following list of words: *bitter, stench, smoky, moldy, coarse, thunderhead, rainbow, wind, smooth, squawk, rasp, silky, raucous, straight, gritty, chatter, salty, rancid, magenta, icy, sour,* *wailing, sweet.* Ask what sense or senses come to mind for each word. Then have your child sort the words into groups. Encourage your child to explain how he or she organized them and why some words fit in more than one group.

This Is to That as These Are to Those

Teach or review with your child that an analogy is a comparison between two pairs of words that are alike in some way. To complete an analogy, one must figure out the relationship between the first pair of words. Take turns writing analogies such as the ones that follow for different family members to solve.

Blue is to sky as _____ is to grass. (green)

Dad is to son as _____ is to daughter. (mom)

Brake is to stop as _____ is to steer. (wheel)

Glove is to hand as shoe is to _____. (foot)

Frame is to picture as fence is to _____. (yard)

Clock is to time as compass is to _____. (direction)

What Does This Word Mean?

When your child encounters unknown words in reading, have him or her follow these steps to decipher them:

1. **Use context clues.** What is the meaning of the other words and sentences around it?

2. **Use structural analysis.** Can you find a base word within it? Do you recognize a prefix or suffix? Can you tell if the word is a present tense or past tense verb?

4. **Look it up in a dictionary.** Is there more than one definition? Can you tell by the context which definition matches? Can you understand the dictionary's explanation?

3. **Ask someone.** Does anyone else in the family know the word?

Help your child recognize that thinking about the context is critical to understanding a word since many words have multiple meanings.

Language Arts for Fourth Graders

Language—writing, speaking, and reading—plays a vital role in all our lives. Without language it would be difficult to express our wants and needs and our feelings and emotions. In the fourth grade, children continue to broaden, fine tune, and strengthen the language skills they need to be effective learners and communicators, orally and in writing. The following skill areas and skills are reinforced in this book:

GRAMMAR AND PARTS OF SPEECH

* nouns, verbs, adjectives, adverbs, pronouns
* interjections

CAPITALIZATION, PUNCTUATION, AND USAGE

* capitalize the beginning of a sentence
* capitalize proper nouns
* capitalize the greeting and the closing in a letter
* end punctuation—period, question mark, exclamation mark
* quotation marks
* apostrophe in contractions
* commas in a friendly letter or business letter
* colon
* italicizing or underlining titles
* homophones (words that sound alike, but have different spellings and, meanings)

WRITING AND PENMANSHIP

* expanding sentences
* spelling words correctly
* letter writing
* taking messages
* writing directions
* writing stories
* writing neatly
* cursive alphabet styles

CAPITALIZING AND PUNCTUATING SENTENCES

The boy hopped.

The <u>silly little</u> boy hopped. (adjectives)

The silly little boy <u>hopped over the fence</u>. (prepositional phrase)

The silly little boy hopped over the <u>wooden</u> fence. (adjective)

The silly little boy <u>quickly</u> hopped over the wooden fence. (adverb)

The silly little boy and <u>his kitten</u> quickly hopped over the wooden fence. (pronoun, noun)

The silly little boy and his kitten quickly hopped over the wooden fence and <u>ran through the meadow</u>. (verb, prepositional phrase)

Sentence Addition

Write this simple sentence on a sheet of paper: *The boy [or girl] hopped.* Take turns adding adjectives, adverbs, nouns, verbs, and prepositional phrases to expand the sentence as much as you can. Be creative and have fun. Your child might also enjoy illustrating the final sentence.

Beginnings and Endings

Does your child know how sentences are supposed to begin and end? Try this activity to reinforce capitalization and punctuation skills. Copy a brief paragraph from a children's book or magazine with two minor changes—use lowercase letters to begin each sentence and omit all end punctuation marks. Be sure to leave a space between writing lines so there is room for corrections. Challenge your child to read the paragraph and determine where each sentence should begin and end. Have your child write capital letters where they belong and add the correct end punctuation. You may want to reveal how many sentences there are altogether in the paragraph. Remind your child to look for other clues such as quotation marks and words that are frequently used to begin question sentences such as who, what, where, why, when, and how.

Here are some books your child may enjoy that involve parts of speech, language exploration, and writing activities for children:

BOOKS TO LOOK FOR

Behind the Mask: A Book About Prepositions by Ruth Heller (Grosset & Dunlap, 1995) [One in a series of books by Heller on parts of speech]

Checking Your Grammar by Marvin Terban (Scholastic, 1993)

It Figures!: Fun Figures of Speech by Marvin Terban (Clarion, 1993)

The Kingfisher Book of Words: A–Z Guide to Quotations, Proverbs, Origins, Usage and Idioms by George Beal (Kingfisher, 1992)

Sincerely Yours: How to Write Great Letters by Carol Barkin and Elizabeth James (Clarion, 1993)

MORE PUNCTUATION ACTIVITIES

Put Them Together— Contractions

Play a contraction game. The first player writes a contraction—two words combined to make a new word with an apostrophe taking the place of the missing letters. The second player writes next to it the two words that made up the contraction. He or she then writes another contraction using one of the two words plus a new word. Continue with each player deciphering the contraction and creating a new one.

Contraction	Two Words
I've	I have
haven't	have not
wouldn't	would not
who'd	who would
who's	who has
she's	she has
she'll	she will
he'll	he will

Something's Coming— Colon

Fourth graders learn that a colon is used in a sentence to signal that a list of items will follow. Write a colon (:) on a scrap of paper and ask your child to identify the punctuation mark. Then copy this sentence:

This is what I have to do after school practice the piano, do my homework, and set the table for supper.

See if your child knows where to place the colon, helping him or her as needed. (The colon follows the word *school.*) Then take turns writing fun sentences that require a colon.

If I could design a new city pool, it would have these things: a high dive, a waterfall, a pirate ship, and 10 different water slides.

What Are They Saying?—Quotation Marks

Invite your child to look through magazines for an interesting picture of two people (or animals) engaged in a conversation. Talk about who they are, what they are doing, and what they might be saying to one another. Then choose parts and take turns writing their conversation, remembering to use quotation marks around each speaker's words. When you have finished, read aloud the conversation with each person reading the lines he or she wrote.

A New Slant on Things

Show this list of titles to your child.

<u>New York Times</u>
New York Times
<u>Ranger Rick</u>
Ranger Rick
<u>Batman Forever</u>
Batman Forever
<u>Pippi Longstocking</u>
Pippi Longstocking
<u>Mona Lisa</u>
Mona Lisa

Have your child identify which is the name of a magazine, a book, a painting, a newspaper, and a movie. Point out that such titles are underlined when handwritten or typed in italics when done on a computer. Ask your child to answer each of these questions in a complete sentence and underline each title:

* What is the name of your local newspaper?
* What magazines do you like to read?
* What is your favorite book?
* What is the last movie you saw?

PARTS OF SPEECH

Mixed-Up Moose—A Past-Tense Verb Game

Most verbs are made past tense by adding -ed. Verbs that do not follow this rule are known as irregular verbs. For example, *asked* is the past tense of *ask,* but *told* is the past tense of *tell.* Practice making verbs past tense by playing a game. The first player tells what Mixed-Up Moose did, using an incorrect verb. The next player tells what Perfect Porcupine did, using the correct verb. Then switch parts.

Example:
Mixed-up Moose runned to the store.
Perfect Porcupine ran to the store.

Here are some verbs you may want to use:

bring come feed have win pay
say find hear read put teach
bite dig flee hold break ride
throw do fly draw forget know
write buy weave drink get leave
stick weep catch drive give lose
take swim eat go see choose

Yikes!

Wow! Zowie! Ow! Good grief! Great! Yippy! Oh no! Teach or review with your child that these words are interjections, or words "thrown in" or interjected into conversations and writing to express feelings or emotions. They might be moans and groans or cheers and hurrahs. Take turns saying or writing interjections you might use in these situations:

* you miss the schoolbus
* you lose a five-dollar bill
* you win a soccer match
* you suddenly feel sick
* you slip and fall in the mud
* you jump into a pool of cold water
* you get an A on a test

Quickly, Quietly, and Often

Adverbs tell where, when, how, how much, or how long. Does your child know that many adverbs, but not all, end in -ly? Your child should also know that adverbs act on verbs, other adverbs, and adjectives. Examples:

	verb	*adverb*
He	ran	quickly.

	adverb	*adjective*
I'm	very	happy.

	verb	*adverb*	*adverb*		
I	can	run	more	quickly	than you.

"Go" on an adverb hunt. Have your child pick a chapter from a book he or she is reading and together look for adverbs. Use the questions below to help decide when you aren't sure. Happy hunting!

* What word is being described? (Remember adverbs never modify a noun or pronoun.)
* Does the word tell where, when, how, how much, or how long?

VOCABULARY AND USAGE

Me or I, First or Last?

Does your child ever start sentences with *Me and . . .*? Teach your child that it is polite to name oneself last. Once you've tackled that half of the problem, you can work on *and me* versus *and I*. The easiest way to figure out which pronoun to use is to rethink the sentence. If the other person or people weren't in it, which would make sense—*me* or *I*?

Wrong: Me and David want to go to the park.

Wrong: David and me want to go to the park.

Wrong: Me want to go to the park.

Right: I want to go to the park.

Right: David and I want to go to the park.

Wrong: Will you take me and David, please?

Wrong: Will you take David and I, please?

Wrong: Will you take I, please?

Right: Will you take me, please?

Right: Will you take David and me, please?

You may need to remind your child 100 times. But eventually he or she will prefer speaking correctly to hearing your corrections!

Homophones

Homophones are words that sound alike, but have different spellings and meanings. Examples: *ate, eight; aisle, isle, I'll*

Brainstorm a list of homophones with your child. Can you think of more than 50? The homophones found in the box on the right are commonly misused by students in their writing. You may want your child to cut out the box to keep at his or her workspace for a handy reference. For additional practice, invite your child to complete "Don't Be Confused" on page 75.

Write It Right!

there	a place; also used as an introductory word *There is a surprise over there.*
their	belongs to them *Their dog had puppies.*
they're	they are *They're so cute!*
to	toward, direction; also used before a verb *A puppy scampered over to me.* *I wanted to play with it.*
too	extreme; also *The puppy was too little.* *It was tired, too.*
two	the number 2 *It napped for two hours.*
its	belongs to it *The puppy chased its tail.*
it's	it is *It's fun to watch the puppy play.*

SPELLING

Name That Rule!

Write the examples for spelling rules below on separate index cards. Then challenge your child to write the spelling rule for each one. The rules are given below each box.

Adjectives

old	older	oldest
fast	faster	fastest
gray	grayer	grayest
big	bigger	biggest
sad	sadder	saddest
happy	happier	happiest
angry	angrier	angriest

* To change most adjectives to ones that compare, add -er and -est.
* When a one-syllable word ends in a short vowel and one consonant, double the final consonant before adding -er and -est.
* When an adjective ends in a consonant and *y*, change the *y* to *i* before adding -er or -est.

Verbs

look	looking	looked
jump	jumping	jumped
skip	skipping	skipped
hum	humming	hummed
play	playing	played
enjoy	enjoying	enjoyed
try	trying	tried
study	studying	studied

* To change most verbs, add -ing or -ed.
* When a one-syllable word ends in a short vowel and one consonant, double the final consonant before adding -ing or -ed.
* When a verb ends in a vowel and *y*, add -ing and -ed as usual.
* When a verb ends in a consonant and *y*, leave the *y* when adding -ing because the ending begins with an *i*. Change the *y* to *i* before adding -ed.

Plural Nouns

solid	solids	gas	gases
comb	combs	brush	brushes
ocean	oceans	beach	beaches
cube	cubes	box	boxes

* Add -s to make most nouns plural.
* Add -es to words that end in s, sh, ch, or x.

Plural Nouns

day	days	sky	skies
toy	toys	baby	babies
guy	guys	lady	ladies
key	keys	fly	flies

* When a noun ends in a vowel and *y*, add -s to make it plural.
* When it ends in a consonant and *y*, change the *y* to *i* and add -es.

Silent e Words

skate	skating	skated
joke	joking	joked
nice	nicer	nicest
rude	ruder	rudest

* If a word ends with silent e, drop the e before adding an ending that begins with a vowel. Examples: -ing, -ed, -er, -est

I Before E?

Teach your child this spelling rhyme:

I before **e** except after **c**, and when sounding like **a** as in *neighbor* and *weigh*.

Here are examples that follow the rule: *yield, belief, achieve, receive, receipt, eight, rein.* Exceptions: *height, either, neither, weird.* Challenge your child to list other rule followers or rule breakers.

CREATIVE WRITING

Dear Sir or Madam:

Letter writing is a skill that combines almost every facet of writing. Talk about the different kinds of correspondence your family sends and receives, such as business letters, invitations, thank-you notes, and letters from friends. Gather and compare examples. Ask questions such as these:

✳ How is a friendly letter different from a business letter?

✳ What words are capitalized in a letter?

✳ What words are abbreviated?

✳ When do you use commas?

✳ When do you use a colon (:)?

✳ What closings might you use for a friendly letter? for a business letter?

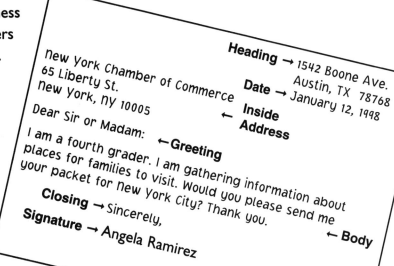

Heading → 1542 Boone Ave. Austin, TX 78768
Date → January 12, 1998

New York Chamber of Commerce
65 Liberty St.
New York, NY 10005

← Inside Address

Dear Sir or Madam: ←Greeting

I am a fourth grader. I am gathering information about places for families to visit. Would you please send me your packet for New York City? Thank you. ← Body

Closing → Sincerely,

Signature → Angela Ramirez

Encourage your child to write a business letter to request information or materials. Guide your child as needed to make sure it is written neatly and correctly. For addresses of organizations and companies offering free or inexpensive materials, check in the latest edition of the book *Free Stuff for Kids* (Meadowbrook Press). Many states and cities have visitors bureaus that will send pamphlets or maps. Check in the current almanac for addresses.

Treasure Hunt

For fun, hide a token gift somewhere in or around your home. Then write a series of directions with clues to help your child find the hidden item. Encourage your child to write a set of treasure hunt clues for a friend or sibling. Follow up by having your child use "Step by Step" on page 76 to practice writing directions for making something.

Look Before You Leap

Ask your child what he or she thinks the proverb "look before you leap" means. Talk about what can happen when you do things without thinking about the consequences. As a family, brainstorm a list of proverbs and discuss what each means. Then rewrite them and compare your versions. Examples:

✳ The grass is always greener on the other side of the fence.

✳ You can lead a horse to water, but you can't make it drink.

✳ Half a loaf is better than none.

✳ A penny saved is a penny earned.

PENMANSHIP

Most children learn cursive handwriting in third grade. They are usually required to use it in fourth grade in order to practice the skill. There are two major styles of cursive handwriting—both are included here for your reference. Check with your child's teacher to see which style your school uses.

Aa Bb Cc Dd Ee Ff
Gg Hh Ii Jj Kk Ll
Mm Nn Oo Pp Qq Rr
Ss Tt Uu Vv Ww Xx
Yy Zz

Aa Bb Cc Dd Ee Ff
Gg Hh Ii Jj Kk Ll
Mm Nn Oo Pp Qq Rr
Ss Tt Uu Vv Ww Xx
Yy Zz

ORAL LANGUAGE

A Day in the Life of . . .

Invite your child and other family members to combine their imagination, knowledge, sense of humor, and speaking skills. Here's how. Write the following inanimate household objects on index cards or any others you want to include:

* toothbrush
* a pair of slippers
* rocking chair
* hammer
* bathroom mirror
* washing machine
* front door welcome mat
* the kitchen garbage can

Put the cards in a bag. Gather family members together and have everyone pick a card. Each person will pretend to be that object and take turns telling about an amusing incident, describing a typical day, or explaining how it feels to be that object. Allow family members a minute or so to think about what to say before standing in front of everyone to speak. If you have a tape recorder or video camera, record each person's speech to play back and enjoy.

Tell Me a Story

Nothing beats a scary ghost story. Have your child find one that he or she particularly likes and read it dramatically to the family. Then talk about what makes it so scary and what it might be like to "run into" a ghost. Challenge your child to write a ghost story. Family members may wish to collaborate. Have your child use "Organize a Scary Story" on page 77 to help plan it. If you have a tape recorder, suggest that your child record sound effects for his or her story, such as a gasp, a knock at the door, or a creaky floorboard. After finishing the story, have your child share it with the family.

What a Voice!

This is another fun activity for the entire family. On separate slips of paper, write different voices like these and place them in a bowl: *scared, angry, weepy, impatient, Southern accent (or British, Caribbean, French . . .), a monster, a tiny fairy, a spy.* Choose a simple poem or a page from a picture book to read. Have each person pull a slip from the bowl and read the excerpt using the voice listed.

Take a Message

Help your child improve his or her oral communication skills while practicing how to take messages at the same time. First talk about the importance of speaking clearly and listening carefully. Next explain what information a message should include. Look at a message pad if you have one. Then role play, taking turns being the caller and the message taker.

> Mom,
> Please call Mrs. Ryan about the soccer game.
> Tom

Mathematics for Fourth Graders

Understanding and applying mathematical skills and concepts is essential in today's world. During fourth grade, much instruction focuses on the mastery of multiplication and division facts and the relationship between the two operations. Children also continue to explore place value, geometry, measurement, decimals, and fractions. Skills for Success for Your Fourth Grader provides activities and suggestions to reinforce the following skills and skill areas:

NUMBERS

* reading and writing numbers in the millions
* expanded notation
* comparing numbers
* rounding to the nearest ten, hundred, and thousand
* Roman numerals

OPERATIONS

* addition and subtraction of multi-digit numbers
* multiplication facts
* division problems
* division with one-digit quotients
* mental math

MEASUREMENT

* U.S. customary units
* metric units
* volume
* estimating capacity

TIME AND MONEY

* problem solving with time and time zones
* U.S. coins and bills
* problem solving involving money

DECIMALS AND FRACTIONS

* decimals to the thoundandths
* common fractions
* equivalent fractions

GEOMETRY

* angles: right $\llcorner$, acute $\angle$, obtuse $\diagdown\llcorner$
* geometric shapes
* ordered pairs

PLACE VALUE

Something of Value

Can your child explain what the term place value means? If not, point out that the value of each digit in a numeral depends on its place, or position. Draw this frame on a piece of paper:

___,___ ___ ___,___ ___ ___

6,741,539

Challenge your child to write each digit of a numeral in the correct place as you read these clues: five hundreds; six millions; nine ones; one thousand; four ten-thousands; three tens; seven hundred-thousands. Continue taking turns narrating or writing numbers. You may want to move on to billions or even trillions! (one trillion = 1,000,000,000,000) Your child may find it useful to refer to a chart like this to help remember place value names when reading and writing large numbers.

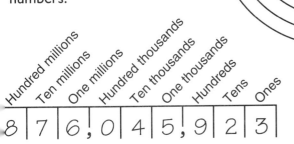

Hundred millions	Ten millions	One millions	Hundred thousands	Ten thousands	One thousands	Hundreds	Tens	Ones
8	7	6,	0	4	5,	9	2	3

Reading Statistics

Look through an almanac or encyclopedia and practice reading big numbers. Take turns finding, writing, and reading aloud the answers to questions like these:

* What is the population of the United States?
* What is the population of China?
* What is the height of Mount Everest?
* How deep is the Mariana Trench?
* How long is the Amazon River?
* How old are the Pyramids?

Target Practice

Make and play a game to reinforce your child's understanding of expanded notation and place value. You'll need a large piece of cardboard, a ruler, a marker, and 20 pennies or paper clips. Make a bullseye like the one shown here:

Take turns tossing all the coins or clips onto the target and using expanded notation to record the score. For example, the score for the clips shown here would be 2,000,000 + 500,000 + 3,000 + 600 + 40 = 2,503,640.

BOOKS TO LOOK FOR

Arithmetricks: 50 Easy Ways to Add, Subtract, Multiply & Divide Without a Calculator by Edward H. Julius (John Wiley & Sons, 1995)

Family Math by Jean Kerr Stenmark (Lawrence Hall of Science, 1986)

Janice VanCleave's Geometry for Every Kid by Janice VanCleave (John Wiley & Sons, 1994)

Math Fun: Test Your Luck by Rose Wyler (Julian Messner, 1992)

Here are some books your child may enjoy that involve math concepts, activities, and tricks for children.

Math Tricks, Puzzles & Games by Raymond Blum (Sterling, 1994)

Math Wizardry for Kids by Margaret Kenda (Barron's, 1995)

NUMBERS AND NUMBER SENSE

Comparing Numbers— Is it > or < ?

Invite your child to write ten pairs of numbers on a sheet of paper, leaving a space between the two. Explain that each pair must have an equal number of digits. Examples:

86 49   709 736
4,827 5,621

Have your child compare each set of numbers and fill in the space with a less than (<) or greater than (>) sign. Remind your child as needed that you compare the digits in the greatest place first. If they are equal, like the hundreds in the second example, you move one place to the right and then compare. If your child confuses the two symbols, point out that the open end always points to the greater number. Some kids like to think of the sign as a shark's mouth

wanting to gobble up the greater number. Conclude the activity by playing a guessing game. Choose one of the numbers. Have your child ask questions involving greater than or less than to figure out which number it is. Examples: *Is it less than 100? Is it greater than 730? Is it less than 4,000?*

Round Up and Round Down

Brainstorm a list of everyday experiences of rounding numbers up or down. Examples: when someone asks you the time, when you give your age, when you measure the length of an item. As you come across numbers in reading, shopping, traveling, and so on, help your child get a feel for the number and how much it is. (That is what teachers mean when referring to *number sense*.) For example, if a new bike costs $186, ask your child if that's about $100 or $200 he or she needs to earn.

Roman Numerals

Ask your child where Roman numerals are sometimes seen today—the face of a clock, the introductory pages of a book, ending credits of a movie, the cornerstone of a building, or chapter numbers in a book. Read the numerals on the chart. See if your child knows these two rules:

✳ When a smaller numeral follows a greater one, you add. XII: 10 + 2 = 12
✳ When a smaller numeral comes before a greater one, you subtract it.
  2XL: 50 − 10 = 40

For fun, have your child use Roman numerals to write the age of each family member, the number of pages in a favorite book, or the year he or she was born.

Roman Numerals

I — 1
II — 2
III — 3
IV — 4
V — 5
VI — 6
VII — 7
VIII — 8
IX — 9
X — 10
XI — 11
XII — 12
XIII — 13
XIV — 14
XV — 15
XVI — 16
XVII — 17
XVIII — 18
XIX — 19
XX — 20
XXX — 30
XL — 40
L — 50
LX — 60
LXX — 70
LXXX — 80
XC — 90
C — 100
D — 500
M — 1,000
MDCCLXXVI — 1776
MMI — 2001

ADDITION AND SUBTRACTION

Give Me a Sign

Make up some simple problems that combine addition and subtraction. Then rewrite the problems, omitting the signs. Challenge your child to figure out the missing signs. Here are some examples to help you get started:

9 (+) 7 (-) 3 (=) 13

18 (-) 9 (+) 7 (=) 16

6 (+) 7 (+) 5 (-) 3 (=) 15

Let your child make up some problems for you to try. Then move on to problems that use greater numbers, such as these:

31 (-) 11 (+) 22 (=) 42

800 (+) 400 (+) 500 (-) 300 (=) 1,400

You may want to get the rest of the family involved. Form teams. Give each team the same problems. The first team to solve all the problems correctly wins.

Mental Math Fun

The more your child practices mental calculations, the better he or she will be at them. You can play this game with your family at home or when stuck standing in line somewhere. The first player gives a starting number. The next person says a number to be added or subtracted to it. Everyone does the calculation mentally. Continue in a circle with each person giving a new command. Every few turns someone may call out "Number check!" All players give their current total. If your child has difficulty mentally adding or subtracting 2-digit numbers, teach him or her to work with tens first and then ones. Example: 92 − 53

Think 92 − 50 = 42.

Then 42 − 3 = 39.

Sums and Differences

Help your child find the population of your state and the populations of the four largest cities within it. You may want to substitute your city if it is not one of the four.

Have your child make a table like this to show the information.

Population	
Colorado	3,307,912
Denver	467,610
Colorado Springs	281,140
Aurora	222,103
Boulder	83,312

Then direct your child to calculate the total number of people who live in the four cities. As your child sets up the addition problem, check to see that he or she lines up the columns of numbers beginning with the ones column. Continue by asking your child to explain how to find the total number of people who live in your state, but not in those four cities. (Subtract the combined population of the cities from the state's population.) Guide your child as needed in solving the subtraction problem.

MULTIPLICATION

It is important for your child to master multiplication facts in fourth grade. The "facts" are the 100 basic multiplication problems needed to solve all other problems. Sample facts: 4 x 6 = 24 9 x 2 = 18. Your child needs to know these accurately and instantly. Although the tens, elevens, and twelves times tables are not basic facts, children should learn them in order to easily solve everyday problems.

Just the Facts!

Use "Just the Facts" on page 79 to assess your child's ability. (First make copies of the page so it can be reused for practice or to check progress.)

Assessment—Evaluate how your child did and where he or she needs help, both by checking answers and by talking with your child.

* Was your child able to work quickly?
* Did your child answer all the problems correctly? If not, which problems does your child need to practice?
* If your child missed a problem, did he or she also miss the related fact? For example, a child might miss 6 x 7, but get 7 x 6 correct.

Patterns—Use these questions to focus on patterns found within the multiplication chart:

* What do you get when you multiply an odd number times an odd number? an even times an even? an odd times an even?

* What answer do you get when you multiply any number by 0?
* What answer do get when you multiply any number by 1?
* When you add the digits for each product in the 9s column or row, what sum do you get?

Multiples of 10

Ask your child to solve this problem mentally:

8 x 10,000

If your child is stumped, give this directive: *Whenever you are multiplying a number by a multiple of 10 (10; 100; 1000; 10,000; 100,000; and so on), count the zeros in the multiple of 10 and place them to the right of the other number.*

Examples:

8 x 10,000 = <u>80,000</u>
(Think 8 with 4 zeros.)

26 x 100 = <u>2,600</u>
(Think 26 with 2 zeros.)

Fun Fact Drill

There is more than one way to learn math facts. The more you try, the better you will learn what works for your child:

* reciting times tables each day
* listening to a rock, rap, or country music cassette of math facts
* tape recording your own set of facts
* writing facts using sidewalk chalk, calligraphy pens, watercolors, or dry erase pens
* typing and illustrating facts on the computer
* playing math drill computer games

DIVISION

Division—Multiplication's Partner

Challenge your child to come up with a way to use the multiplication table on page 79 to determine divisors and quotients. If your child needs help figuring it out, suggest that he or she find the dividend 36 near the bottom of the table. Have your child run one finger to the number at the beginning of the row (9) and another finger to the number at the top of the column (4). Explain that $36 \div 9 = 4$, or $36 \div 4 = 9$. Have your child try it with other numbers.

Fact Families

A fact family is a set of related multiplication and division facts. Example:

$3 \times 5 = 15$

$5 \times 3 = 15$

$15 \div 3 = 5$

$15 \div 5 = 3$

Call out three numbers that make up a fact family, such as 3, 5, and 15, and have your child write the problems. You may want your child to draw and describe matching scenarios.

Division Tic Tac Toe

Ask your child to write division fact problems he or she needs to practice on separate index cards. Make a Tic Tac Toe board and gather some pennies and dimes to represent Xs and Os. To play, mix the cards and place them facedown. Take turns drawing a problem card from the pile and solving it. If you get it correct, place one of your coins on the board. The first player to get three across, down, or diagonally wins the round.

$56 \div 7 =$

9
81

Division Tidbits

Point out that you don't always have to write out every step to solve a division problem—sometimes you can solve it mentally. Use 1648 divided by 4 to illustrate.

Think

16 hundreds $\div$ 4 = 4 hundreds, and

4 tens $\div$ 4 = 1 ten, and

8 ones $\div$ 4 = 2 ones.

So without writing out the steps, you can solve the problem.

$$\frac{412}{4 \overline{)1648}}$$

Here's another example to share with your child when dividing two-digit numbers with remainders. Use 85 divided by 2 to illustrate.

Think

85 = 80 + 5, and

80 $\div$ 2 = 40, and

5 $\div$ 2 = 2 R 1.

(R is Remainder)

40 + 2 R 1 = 42 R 1, so

85 $\div$ 2 = 42 R 1.

TIME

What Time Is It?

If it's 9:00 A.M. where you and your family live, what time is it in New York? in San Francisco? in Phoenix? To answer such questions, your child will need a time zone map. If you don't have one, check the front pages of your telephone directory. Then take turns making up questions to challenge one another.

If we want to call Grandma in Florida at 7 p.m. her time, what time should we call?

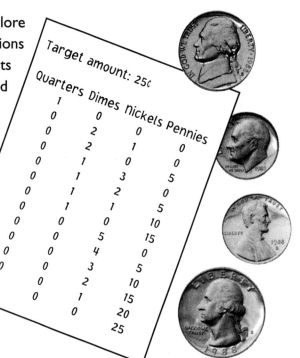

Think Backwards

Many everyday time problems involve thinking backwards. You can help your child practice math while planning activities. Encourage your child to list important information first. For example, What time does your child need to start making the brownies for the concert tonight? Important facts:

* The school concert begins at 7:30 p.m.
* You need to leave by 7:10 p.m. to get good seats.
* Brownies take 15 minutes to mix, 30 minutes to bake, and 2 hours to cool.

A Daily Schedule

Invite your child to write a schedule for a typical Wednesday, noting wakeup time, morning activities, school, lessons or sports, homework, playtime, meals, and bedtime. Use the schedule to solve problems involving time. Example: How much time do you spend sleeping?

MONEY

Combinations

With your child, explore using different combinations of coins to make amounts under a dollar. You'll need pennies, nickels, dimes, and quarters, and a half dollar, if you happen to have one. Keep a chart to record your results. Try a similar activity using paper money and change for amounts up to twenty dollars.

Target amount: 25¢

Quarters	Dimes	Nickels	Pennies
1	0	0	0
0	2	0	0
0	2	1	0
0	1	0	0
0	1	3	5
0	1	2	0
0	1	1	5
0	0	0	10
0	0	5	15
0	0	4	0
0	0	3	5
0	0	2	10
0	0	1	15
0			20
0			25

How Calculating!

The next time you go to the grocery store, invite your child to come along with you. Give your child a calculator and put him or her in charge of comparing prices, finding the total, and checking the change.

Toss and Add

Create a gameboard similar to the one on page 81. Substitute time amounts or dollar and cents amounts to give your child practice adding time or money.

MEASUREMENT

Metric or U.S. Customary Units?

The metric system is used by most major countries of the world, except for the United States. Therefore fourth graders learn to measure using both systems. Brainstorm a list of everyday objects or experiences that involve measurement. Then talk about whether they use U.S. customary units, metric units, or both.

> **Sports**
> football—yards
> track—meters, miles
>
> **Cooking**
> food—ounces, pounds, grams
> beverages—cups, pints, gallons, liters

Measuring Fun—Length

Have your child lie on the ground or on a large sheet of cardboard or paper. Trace his or her outline with a piece of chalk. Next have your child use a ruler to measure the distances in inches or centimeters from head to toe, heel to knee, shoulder to finger tip, top of the head to the shoulder, and so on. Then challenge your child to find the length of the entire chalk line. Extend the activity by having your child convert inches to feet or yards. Or if the measurements were done in centimeters, convert them to meters when possible.

Length Conversions

12 inches	= 1 foot
3 feet	= 1 yard
100 centimeters	= 1 meter

What's the Volume?

Volume is the amount of space an object takes up. Use page 80 to give your child practice calculating the volume of a rectangular prism, such as a box of cereal, a shoe box, or a thick book. Help your child measure and record the length, width, and height of each item to the nearest centimeter or inch. Then use this formula to find the volume:

$$V = l \times w \times h$$

(Volume = length x width x height).

Answers will be in cubic centimeters or cubic inches.

How Much Does It Hold?

Clean and save containers of varying sizes, such as orange juice cans, milk cartons, and shampoo bottles. You will also need measuring cups and pencil and paper. Have your child look at the various containers and estimate how much each holds. You might want your child to choose one unit to focus on, for example, cups. Ask questions such as these: *How many cups does this shampoo bottle hold? How many cups of milk were in this carton?* After writing estimates, have your child use measuring cups filled with water to check.

U.S. Customary Units of Capacity

1 cup	= 8 fluid ounces
1 pint	= 2 cups
1 quart	= 2 pints
1 gallon	= 4 quarts

DECIMALS AND FRACTIONS

Two and four hundredths, 2.04, 2⁴⁄₁₀₀

Make sets of cards with decimals written in three forms—as words, decimals, and fractions. Use the cards as flash cards or to play a memory match game. To play the game, place all cards facedown. Take turns picking and reading aloud three cards. If they match, keep the set and take another turn. If not, return the cards facedown. The player with the most sets wins. This graphic might be helpful to your child when reading and writing decimals.

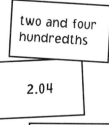

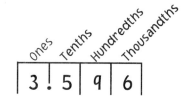

Decimal Riddles

Practice decimals with riddles like this one:
Use the digits 2, 4, 7, and 8. The greatest digit is in the hundredths place.
The digit in the tenths place is 2 more than the digit in the ones place.
The digit in the thousandths place is 1 less than the digit in the hundredths place.
What is the number?
Answer: 2.487

Toss and Add

Let your child practice adding decimals by playing the game on page 81. You can also use it to practice subtracting decimals. Players start with the number 100 and subtract the scores of each of their five tosses. The lowest number wins. Make sure your child lines up the decimal points before adding or subtracting.

Double Batch and Half Batch

When you need to adjust a recipe, involve your child in calculating the changes in the

amount required of each ingredient. Let your child solve the problems using either paper and pencil or measuring cups and spoons.

Fraction Fold

You'll need four same-size sheets of plain paper and some crayons to do this activity. Have your child position the paper as shown in the sketches and color the bottom parts. After each step, have your child tell the total number of parts, the value of each part, and how many parts are shaded.

1. Fold the first sheet in half lengthwise. Color one part.

2. Fold the second sheet in half lengthwise, and then in half again. Color 2 parts.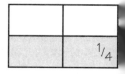

3. Fold the third sheet in half lengthwise, and then in thirds. Color 3 parts.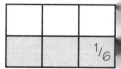

4. Fold the fourth sheet in half lengthwise. Then fold it in half two more times. Color 4 parts.

Line up all four sheets so that your child sees that 1/2, 2/4, 3/6, and 4/8 are equivalent.

GEOMETRY

What's Your Angle?

Teach or review with your child that a right angle forms a square corner (90°), an acute angle is less than a right angle, and an obtuse angle is greater than a right angle. Then together look for examples of each angle around your home. Make a three-column chart to record your observations. If you have trouble finding acute and obtuse angles, consider the angles formed by a hinged photo frame, a partially opened door, the hands on a clock, a design in a painting, or a missing piece of pie.

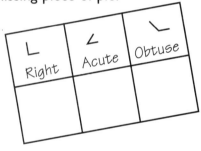

Parallel or Perpendicular?

The next time you take a neighborhood walk, look for parallel and perpendicular lines. For example, a telephone pole is perpendicular to the road, while the curb in front of your home and the curb on the opposite side of the street are parallel to each other.

Four Sides

Does your child know what a quadrilateral is? The prefix *quadri-* means "four" and *lateral* comes from the Latin word for "side"—quadrilaterals are four-sided shapes. Challenge your child to draw or use toothpicks to make different quadrilaterals. Which of the quadrilaterals shown did your child create? Can your child describe the quadrilaterals using some of these terms: equal, unequal, opposite sides, parallel, right angles?

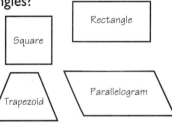

Shapes Making Shapes

For fun, have your child draw and cut out a large trapezoid. Then pose this challenge: *Show how you can cut the trapezoid into three pieces which when rearranged will make a parallelogram and a rectangle.* Solution:

Drawing the Line

Have your child draw a 6-inch square and then within it draw a floor plan to show how he or she would arrange the following items: bed, bookcase, desk, dresser, oval area rug, nightstand, and beanbag chair. Next have your child make a grid by measuring and connecting one-inch intervals on all four sides. Direct your child to number the lines as shown.

Teach your child that an ordered pair pinpoints a place on the grid. The first number tells how many lines to the right of 0 you move, and the second number tells how many lines up from 0 you move. Call out ordered pairs, such as (2, 4), and have your child name the furniture item drawn there.

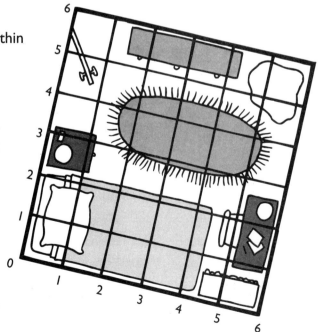

Science for Fourth Graders

Science offers children a wonderful opportunity to explore, discover, and learn—not just through reading but through observations and hands-on experiences as well. Each school or school district has its own guidelines of which topics will be covered in fourth grade. *Skills for Success for Your Fourth Grader* reinforces the following areas:

PHYSICAL SCIENCE

* electricity
* energy conservation
* air and air pressure

EARTH AND SPACE SCIENCE

* weather
* rocks
* sedimentation
* the effects of natural events on the earth
* fossils

* the earth's structure
* solar system
* recycling
* water conservation
* environmental issues

LIFE SCIENCE

* plants
* animals
* ecosystems

* human body
* nutrition

LET'S EXPERIMENT

The next time you visit the library or bookstore, browse through the science activity books and choose one with your child's input. To help you make a choice, consider these factors: how easy or complex the experiments are, the materials required, and the preparation involved. Have fun doing the experiments together. Encourage your child to try to explain what is happening and why it works or doesn't work. You may suggest that your child record the steps, the results, and his or her comments about the experiment in a notebook.

PHYSICAL SCIENCE

Saving Energy

One of the most important forms of energy is electricity. Walk around the house with your child and point out items that use electricity. Talk about ways to save electricity, or energy, such as these:

* turning off the lights, stereo, and TV when they are not being used
* putting on warmer clothes when it is cold instead of turning up the heat
* walking, riding a bike, car pooling or riding the bus
* using the washing machine, dryer, or dishwasher only when it is full
* cleaning the dryer's lint filter after each use

Then have your child conduct a poll among relatives or neighbors to draw attention to the importance of conserving energy. Begin by helping your child develop a set of yes or *no* questions and a way to record the responses, such as a tally sheet. After polling people, talk about the results.

Light as Air

Ask your child if he or she thinks that air has weight. To find out, try a demonstration. You'll need two balloons, string, a hanger, and a pin. Have your child blow up the balloons so both are as equal in size as possible and tie each at opposite ends of the hanger. Have your child hold the hanger on a finger. The balloons should balance each other. Then using the pin, prick one balloon near the top. Ask your child to explain what happens to the hanger and why. (The balloon that is still filled with air weighs more than the empty balloon, and as a result, the hanger is pulled down on that side.)

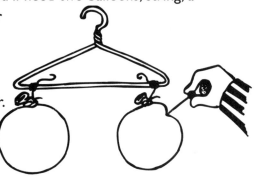

What Pressure!

Remind your child that air not only has weight, but it also pushes and presses in all directions. This pushing and pressing is called air pressure. To show one way that air pressure works, have your child fill a glass bottle with water. Direct your child to put a thumb over the bottle opening, turn the bottle upside down in a pan of water, and take his or her thumb away. What happens to the water in the bottle? (The pressure of air pushing down on the water in the pan holds the water up in the bottle.)

BOOKS TO LOOK FOR

50 Simple Things Kids Can Do to Save the Earth by EarthWorks Group (Andrews McMeel, 1990)

175 Science Experiments to Amuse and Amaze Your Friends by Brenda Walpole (Random House, 1988)

Foodworks by the Ontario Science Centre (Addison-Wesley, 1987)

How Come? by Kathy Wollard (Workman, 1993)

Kids Can Save the Animals! by Ingrid Newkirk (Warner, 1991)

Here are some books your child may enjoy that involve science concepts and activities.

The Kid's Nature Book: 365 Indoor/Outdoor Activities and Experiences by Susan Milord (Williamson, 1989)

WEATHER

Air Pressure and Weather

Here are some key concepts relating to air pressure and weather your child should learn:

✶ Meteorologists use an instrument called a barometer to measure air pressure.

✶ Storms are more likely to occur where air pressure is low.

✶ Differences in air pressure cause wind.

Together study a newspaper weather map. Have your child use the key to find the symbols that represent high pressure and low pressure areas. Look for storms and see if they do occur near low pressure areas.

Dew Drop In

Your child may have learned that water vapor in the air condenses when the air is cooled, forming dew and clouds. To see this process, have your child wipe the outside of an empty tin can so that it is dry and then put several ice cubes and some water in the can. After 10 minutes, ask your child to describe what happens and to explain where the water on the outside of the can came from. Emphasize that it did not come from inside the can. Help your child recognize that as the ice melted, it took heat from the can. As the can cooled, it cooled the air around it causing water in the nearby air to come together as drops.

Cloud Watching

Scientists name and classify clouds based on their appearance, composition, and level in the sky. Read the following words to see if your child recognizes they are names of clouds: cirrus, cumulus, stratus, cumulonimbus. Encourage your child to observe clouds over a few weeks and to identify what kinds they are. Gather reference books as needed. For fun, take a walk together on a partly cloudy day. Watch clouds move across the sky and observe their shapes. Sketch some of the formations, particularly clouds that look like something else.

How's the Weather?

Have your child get the weather forecast from the newspaper, radio, or TV each day for five days. Let him or her keep a weather log on page 83 by recording the date, predicted weather, and how the weather actually turned out each day.

Water From Snow

Does it snow where you live? If so, have your child find out how much water comes from snow. The next time it starts to snow, have your child put a can outside. When the snowfall ends, measure the height of the snow in the can. After the snow melts, have your child then measure the meltwater, or the amount of water from snowfall. Is he or she surprised? Why? Help your child conclude that it takes a lot of snow to make a little water. Encourage your child to think about why meltwater is important to people and why it is sometimes dangerous.

EARTH SCIENCE

Rock Hunt

Your child has probably learned there are three main categories of rocks:

* Igneous rock is formed when melted rock inside the earth's crust cools and hardens.
* Sedimentary rock is formed from sediment, such as mud, sand, and gravel, that settles in layers at the bottom of lakes and oceans and then hardens into rock. It often contains fossils.
* Metamorphic rock is formed from igneous and sedimentary rocks that are chemically changed by heat and pressure deep within the crust.

Have your child collect rocks in your neighborhood and then use reference books to identify them. If you have a magnifying glass, have your child look for the visible physical properties of each.

Fossil Finds

A fossil is a remnant or trace of a plant or animal from long ago embedded and preserved in a rock. The next time you visit a science museum or natural history museum, see if there is a fossil exhibit. You may even be able to find examples of fossils in the rocks at a nearby park. Take photographs and make some rubbings if you do.

Have your child make his or her own fossils. You'll need a pan or tray, plaster of paris, vegetable oil, water, a spoon, and five small objects (leaf, bone, shell, section of a branch, flower, and so on). After mixing the plaster with water to form a pastry-like mix, pour it into the pan or tray. Have your child coat the objects with vegetable oil and place them in the plaster. When the plaster begins to harden, direct your child to carefully remove the objects. Talk about the prints and how they are similar to the objects. Then have your child show the tray to other family members to see if they can identify the objects that made them.

Sedimentation in a Jar

To observe sedimentation, have your child complete the activity on page 84. He or she will be mixing soil and water in a large jar and observing how the contents settle. If possible, find a variety of items to mix in with your backyard soil—clay, sand, pebbles, and so on. Your child should discover that the contents settle in layers with the heavier items at the bottom.

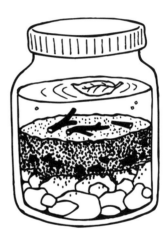

The Changing Earth

To reinforce the idea that the earth is changing, ask your child to identify some of the natural events and disasters that indicate this, such as earthquakes, volcanic eruptions, tsunamis, tornadoes, hurricanes, floods, and erosion. Look around the area where you live for examples of changes. Invite your child to research a natural event, such as the 1980 eruption of Mount St. Helens.

EARTH AND SPACE

The Core of the Matter

The next time you are about to eat an apple, cut out a wedge and show the apple to your child. Explain how an apple is like the earth. The crust is like the apple skin. It is the outer layer of rock that covers the earth. The mantle is like the white part of the apple. It is the thickest layer of the earth. The earth's core is like an apple core. It is the innermost part. Make a list of related questions your child is curious about. Then help your child find the answers. Sample questions:

✳ How far into the earth have humans been able to reach?

✳ How deep is the mantle? What is it made of?

✳ How hot is the core of the earth?

Internet Resources

If you have Internet access, explore these websites with your child:

✳ **StarChild**
http://heasarc.gsfc.nasa.gov/docs/StarChild/

✳ **NASA Spacelink**
http://spacelink.msfc.nasa.gov/home.index.html

✳ **The Nine Planets**
http://seds.lpl.arizona.edu/billa/tnp/

Let's See

Enliven your child's study of the solar system with these nighttime family activities:

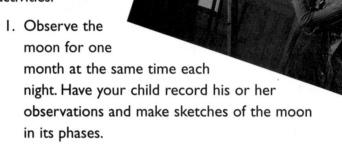

1. Observe the moon for one month at the same time each night. Have your child record his or her observations and make sketches of the moon in its phases.

2. Look for notices about upcoming lunar and solar eclipses and where they can be observed. Then watch the events together. Encourage your child to record his or her observations and to jot down questions to research later.

3. Look for and identify constellations.

4. Try to locate Mercury, Venus, Mars, Jupiter, or Saturn on a clear night.

5. Visit a nearby planetarium or observatory. Study the night sky through a telescope.

Dough Models

Challenge your child to do some research to find the structure of different planets. For example, Mercury is believed to have a large iron core, a medium-thin mantle, and a thin crust around it. Neptune is thought to have a small core surrounded by a thick ocean of water and gases, and then an atmosphere of gases around it. You may want to look for these books with their excellent color diagrams:

The Children's Space Atlas by Robin Kerrod (Millbrook Press, 1992)

The Visual Dictionary of the Universe (Dorling Kindersley, 1993)

Then gather different colors of clay or play dough. Let your child use them to make models of the different planets. Direct your child to roll a ball to make a planet's core. Then have your child choose other colors to make the surrounding layers. He or she can slice the finished planets in half to view their interiors.

ENVIRONMENTAL TOPICS

An Acid Rain Experiment

When water vapor mixes with chemical pollutants in the air, it causes the rain, snow, and fog to be more acidic. To show the effects of acid rain on plants, your child will need two identical house-plants, water, and vinegar. Have your child water the plants for three weeks, one with water and the other with water mixed with a few teaspoons of vinegar. Direct your child to record his or her observations. Discuss the results (a dying plant) and the implications for plant life on a large scale.

Recycle It

Hold a family discussion about the importance of recycling and what each family member can do to help. For one week, have your child list all the things he or she throws away. Review the list together and check for items that could have been recycled, such as aluminum cans, notebook paper, or old clothes.

Water Conservation

Share these water facts with your family:

✳ a five-minute shower uses about 25 gallons

✳ a bath uses about 50 gallons

✳ flushing the toilet uses 3 to 5 gallons of water

✳ running the washing machine uses 30 gallons

✳ running the dishwasher uses 10 gallons

Have your child keep a log of all the times he or she uses water in a day. If you live in an area where water conservation is an issue, discuss ways your family can conserve. Examples:

Don't leave the water running when brushing your teeth or washing dishes; repair leaky faucets; keep a bottle of drinking water in the refrigerator so you don't have to run the water waiting for it to get cold.

Help!

Many children are concerned about environmental issues, such as pollution, endangered species, acid rain, litter, global warming, and damage to the ozone. If your child feels strongly about one of these issues or a community concern, help him or her explore different ways to get involved. You may wish to have your child write to these or other organizations:

U.S. Environmental Protection Agency
Office of External Relations and Education
Youth Programs (A-108)
401 M Street, SW
Washington, DC 20460

World Wildlife Fund
1250 24th Street, NW
Washington, DC 20037

The Center for Marine Conservation
1725 De Sales Street NW, Suite 500
Washington, DC 20036

Recycle!

PLANTS AND ANIMALS

A Nursery Field Trip

Skim through kids' gardening books to introduce your child to some plant basics. Then take your child to a nearby nursery where a wide variety of plants can be observed. Read the labels to see what they need in terms of sunlight, water, and temperature. Ask someone to help you learn which plants grow well in your climate and any interesting tidbits they know about the different plants. Let your child buy something to plant and care for. If you do not have space for a garden, perhaps your child could have a large pot on a porch or balcony.

Take a Cutting

See if your child can get a new plant to grow from a cutting. Coleus, geraniums, philodendrons, pussy willows, and forsythias work well. After taking a cutting, have your child cut through the stem on an angle just below a leaf and place it in a jar of water, carefully removing any leaves that are under the water. Keep the jar on a windowsill where it can get some sun. Have your child check the plant each day, adding water as necessary, and noting any changes. When it has developed roots, help your child pot it in soil.

What's In Your Ecosystem?

An ecosystem is a community of living and non-living things that interact. For example, a forest, a tidepool, and your neighborhood are each ecosystems. Discuss the living and nonliving things that make up your neighborhood ecosystem. Then have your child draw a map that shows the area in which you live and some of the ecosystems found in that environment. Remind your child to include a map key.

Build a Better Bird's Nest?

Try to find a fallen or abandoned bird's nest for your child and other family members to observe. Talk about the materials that the birds used to make the nest— mud, twigs, grass, string, yarn, and so on. Then have family members gather similar materials and each try to construct a bird's nest like the one they've observed. Everyone will probably have a much greater appreciation for the ability of feathered creatures to construct nests.

How Observant!

Have your child identify wildlife that is common to your area, such as chipmunks, lizards, or seagulls. Invite your child to choose one kind of animal to observe periodically at different times of the day to discover more about its habits and behavior. Suggest using binoculars to get a better look. Direct your child to record observations in a notebook, organizing the information as shown.

My observations of
Physical characteristics
Sounds they make
What they eat
How they get their food
Interesting behavior

HUMAN BODY

Healthful Eating

Talk to your child about the food guide pyramid on page 85. Discuss the different food groups, the suggested daily servings for each, and how much food is in a serving. Here's a chart to help you.

Milk, Yogurt, and Cheese Group
1 serving =   1 cup milk or yogurt or 1½ to 2 oz. cheese

Meat, Poultry, Fish, Dry Beans, Eggs, and Nuts Group
1 serving =   2 to 3 oz. of cooked meat, fish,
              or poultry
              or 1 to 1½ cups cooked dry beans
              or 2 eggs
              or 4 to 6 T peanut butter

Vegetable Group
1 serving =   1 cup raw, leafy vegetables
              or ½ cup other vegetables
              (cooked or raw)
              or ¾ cup vegetable juice

Fruit Group
1 serving =   1 medium apple, banana,
              or orange or ½ cup cooked, chopped,
              or canned fruit or ¾ cup fruit juice

Bread, Cereal, Rice, and Pasta Group
1 serving =   1 slice of bread
              or 1 oz. ready-to-eat cereal
              or ½ cup cooked cereal, rice,
              or pasta

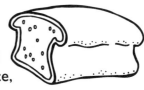

Creating Balanced Meals

Have your child help plan the family dinner menu for four nights. Tell your child that each meal he or she plans must have a food from each of the four basic food groups (milk, meat, fruit and vegetable, and bread and cereal). Have your child draw four equal-sized circles on a sheet of paper and label each circle with one of the food groups. Then have him or her divide each circle into four equal parts. Next have your child draw a picture in each section of a circle that represents a food from that circle's food group. For example in the milk group circle, he or she might draw pictures of milk, cheese, yogurt, and cottage cheese. Have your child do the same thing for each of the circles.

Then have him or her cut the circles into fourths. Finally have your child create new circles by selecting a picture from each food group and gluing the pictures together to form circles. The new circles will serve as the menus for balanced meals since they will each have one item from each food group represented.

Social Studies for Fourth Graders

In the fourth grade, children learn about areas that are beyond their own neighborhoods and communities and they begin to focus on their own states, regions, and the entire country. The curriculum is varied, featuring geography, economics, civics and citizenship, culture, and history. *Skills for Success for Your Fourth Grader* presents activities and suggestions for these topics:

GEOGRAPHY

* U.S. states
* continents
* bodies of water
* landforms
* reading maps
* longitude and latitude
* interpreting graphs

ECONOMICS

* natural resources
* budgets

CITIZENSHIP

* national symbols
* local, state, and national leaders
* current events

CULTURE

* cultural diversity
* immigration
* recognizing differences and similarities

HISTORY

* Native Americans
* exploration
* westward movement
* women's history
* civil rights
* comparing the past and present

U.S. GEOGRAPHY

Our Great State

Suppose an out-of-town friend or relative were coming to visit your family and state for two weeks. Where would you take that person? Invite your child to plan a state tour. Have your child gather state maps, travel guides, and brochures. Next direct your child to list landmarks, interesting cities and towns, museums, state parks, and recreational areas that would interest the visitor. Then have your child plan the route, the itinerary, and the method of transportation. Take advantage of your child's research by visiting some of the places with your family.

Mystery State

You'll need a large U.S. map for this family activity. One person gives clues about a state. The other family members study the map to determine the mystery state. Sample: *This state is surrounded by six other states. It borders South Dakota, but not North Dakota. It does not border Colorado. Its capital city is Des Moines.* (Iowa)

Show What You Know

Make several copies of the map on page 86. You can use it in any of these ways, either having your child copy the information from a book or labeling it by memory:

* Label the state names.
* Label state postal abbreviations.
* Label state capitals.
* Label the cities of each NBA team.
* Label and illustrate 10 national parks.
* Label and color the states you've visited.
* Label rivers and mountain ranges.
* Draw symbols for products, resources, or sites states are known for.
* Draw a path showing a vacation you would like to take.
* Label places where your relatives live.

BOOKS TO LOOK FOR

Here are some books your child may enjoy that involve social studies concepts or activities.

Children Just Like Me by Barnabas and Anabel Kindersley (Dorling Kindersley, 1995)

Do People Grow on Family Trees? by Ira Wolfman (Workman Publishing, 1991)

The Great Atlas of Discovery by Neil Grant (Knopf, 1992)

Hands Around the World by Susan Milord (Williamson, 1992)

It Happened in America: True Stories from the Fifty States by Lila Perl (Henry Holt, 1992)

My First Book of Biographies: Great Men and Women Every Child Should Know by Jean Marzollo (Scholastic, 1994)

The World Almanac for Kids (World Almanac, 1995)

WORLD GEOGRAPHY

Where in the World?

As you watch the evening news together or discuss events you've been reading about in newspapers or magazines, check to be sure your child knows where the events are taking place. Using an atlas, a globe, or a world map, challenge your child to locate each place. You may want to provide clues. For example, if your child isn't sure where Israel is, suggest that he or she look along the eastern shore of the Mediterranean Sea.

In the Mail

Encourage your child to start a collection of stamps and postmarks from other states and countries around the world. Have your child find each location on a map or globe. Then direct your child to categorize the items by region or continent and place them in a scrapbook.

Water, Water, Everywhere

You'll need a globe or world map, slips of paper, and a timer for this activity. Begin by talking about the differences between an ocean, sea, lake, and river. Look for examples of each on the map or globe. Then write the names of bodies of water on your slips of paper. Play a family game in which you take turns picking a slip and locating the place on the map or globe. Set a time limit based on each person's ability or experience.

Suggested places:

Arctic Ocean
Pacific Ocean
Atlantic Ocean
Indian Ocean
Nile River
Yangtze River
Congo River
Amazon River
Mississippi River
Rio Grande
Missouri River
Volga River
Caribbean Sea
Mediterranean Sea
Dead Sea
North Sea
Bering Sea
Red Sea
Baltic Sea
Caspian Sea
Lake Superior
Lake Michigan
Great Salt Lake
Lake Baikal
Lake Victoria

Made in America?

You and your child may be surprised to discover where all the things you buy and consume were produced or manufactured. Together, check such things as your appliances, tools, clothing, housewares, food and food products, toys and games, sports equipment, and linens to see where they were made. Have your child make a list of the products and countries. Ask: *Do some countries or does a single country appear more often than others? Which one(s)? Are you surprised?* Discuss the results.

Continent Category Cards

Your family can divide into two teams to play this game. On separate index cards, have everyone write names of famous places, bodies of water, mountains and volcanoes, or countries from around the world. You may want to cut and glue pictures from old magazines to illustrate them. On the back of each card, write the continent where it is found. Mix up the cards and give half to each team. Teams race each other to sort all the cards into piles by continent.

MAPS AND GRAPHS

From Here to There

Study a street map of your community. Discuss the different parts of the map, such as the legend, compass rose, and the index of streets. Then talk about some of the places that are important to your family—the homes of friends and relatives, schools, your work site, your place of worship, the post office, the library, grocery store, and so on. Together locate each place on the map. Then take turns giving each other directions to get from one place to another. Encourage your child to use directional terms, such as north, south, east, west, left, and right.

60°N Latitude 150°W Longitude

Lines of latitude and longitude help one locate places on a map. Have your child use a finger to trace these lines on a world map or globe:

✱ the Equator (0°Latitude)

✱ latitude lines that run parallel to the Equator that are north of it and then south of it

✱ the Prime Meridian which crosses through Greenwich, England (0°Longitude)

✱ longitude lines that run parallel to the Prime Meridian that are east of it and then west of it

Together practice identifying the latitude and longitude of cities and states of the United States. Then play a game with your child. Take turns giving each other intersecting lines of latitude and longitude and identifying where you would be. Examples:

Which state are you in at 35°N latitude and 105°W longitude? (New Mexico)

Which city is at 30°N latitude and 90°W longitude? (New Orleans)

Which city is near 60°N latitude and 150°W longitude? (Anchorage)

Look At This!—Graphs

Have your child look through old newspapers and magazines to find and cut out examples of bar graphs, circle graphs, line graphs, and pictographs. Talk about what each graph shows, how to read the graphs, and why graphs are useful. Your child can create his or her own graph using page 87.

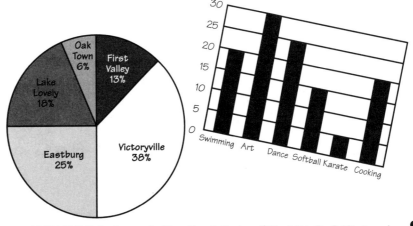

CITIZENSHIP

A Matter of Identity

Recognizing the symbols of the United States of America is one facet of being a knowledgeable citizen. Make up a fun quiz for or with your child. Cut from magazines photographs or illustrations of U.S. symbols, plus other pictures that could be wrong answers.

Sample questions:

Where does the U.S. president live—at the Taj Mahal or the White House?

Which animal is a symbol of the Republican party—an elephant or a rhinoceros?

Which animal is a symbol of the Democratic party—a goat or a donkey?

Which relative is a symbol of our country—Whistler's mother or Uncle Sam?

Which motto is found on U.S. money—*C'est la vie* or *E pluribus unum*?

Which bird is a symbol of our country—a bald eagle or a peacock?

What is *Old Glory*—the U.S. flag or the Statue of Liberty?

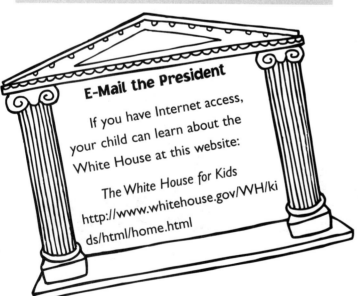

E-Mail the President

If you have Internet access, your child can learn about the White House at this website:

The White House for Kids
http://www.whitehouse.gov/WH/kids/html/home.html

Who Are the Leaders?

Challenge your child to name the current president and vice-president of the United States, the governor of your state, and other important leaders. Help your child become better acquainted with your local government by visiting your City Hall. Or attend a council meeting together to see democracy in action.

Don't Forget to Vote

Be sure to take your child with you when you vote, demonstrating the ballot and procedure. Talk about the candidates and issues before the election. Explain which ones you support and why. Point out differing opinions within your community. Find out if your child's school participates in a children's voting program.

Current Events

Encourage your child to join you as you read the newspaper, listen to the radio, or watch the television news. Involve your child in discussions of current events. A simple question like "What do you think?" will help your child begin to understand that every citizen's opinions are important.

Easy Come and Easy Go

You can introduce your child to the concept of government budgets by talking about a family budget or a budget for your child. Discuss the major activities involving money—earning, saving, and spending. Explain that your family spends money on things you need and things you want. Brainstorm a list of items or services your family has spent money on in the past week. Have your child decide if each is a want or a need. Then let your child choose something he or she wants. Have your child use page 89 as a budget plan.

PEOPLE AND CULTURE

Focus on Your Family

Share your family's history with your child. Are your ancestors Native Americans or did they come from somewhere else? When did they come to America? Where did they come from? Did they immigrate willingly or were they brought here as an enslaved people? If they immigrated, did they enter the United States through Ellis Island? What did they have to do to become citizens? How long did it take? Do you have any old photographs, papers, letters, or passports you could show your child? For fun, help your child make a family tree.

What's Your Last Name, Please?

Do you and your child know the origin of your last name and what it means? For example, Altman is of German origin and means "old man," Allard is of English origin and means "the bald one," Jaffee is of Hebrew origin and means "pretty." Talk about your family's names. Check the library for helpful references, such as *New Dictionary of American Family Names* by Elsdon C. Smith (Harper & Row, 1973).

Food Words

Immigrants bring not only their art, music, dances, and style of dress, but special foods and food words, as well. For example, *hamburger* comes from German, *tomato* from Spanish, and *sherbet* from Arabic. Let your child guess the language these words each come from. Then look them up in a dictionary to check. Your child can use page 90 to record words he or she comes across.

chocolate	spinach
sugar	frankfurter
apricot	tuna
mayonnaise	teriyaki
coffee	minestrone
pretzel	bagel
spaghetti	tortilla
tea	

Dear Pen Pal

What do children in other parts of the world do for fun? What do they study in school? Do they celebrate the same holidays as U.S. families do? What are their homes like? Your child might find it fun and interesting to have a pen pal from another country. It's a great opportunity to practice letter-writing skills while learning about other people and cultures. Here are some organizations to contact:

World Pen Pals
1694 Como Avenue
St. Paul, MN 55108

International Friendship
League
55 Mount Vernon Street
Boston, MA 02108

International Pen Friends
P.O. Box 290065
Brooklyn, NY 11229

Discuss what your child could write about in the first letter—your family; where you live; what he or she likes to do at home, at school, and with friends. Suggest that your child ask some questions, too, and even include a photograph.

The First Americans

Your child probably knows that long before the arrival of Europeans in North America, there were many established societies already living on the continent. They came to be called Indians because Columbus thought he had reached the Indies. What your child might not know is that there are many Indian peoples alive and well today! Together explore the library, historical society, and local museums to learn about Native Americans who lived in your state or region in the past. Then look for powwows, craft or dance demonstrations, storytelling programs, or other events to learn more about Native Americans who currently live in your area.

Westward Ho!

Ask your child to guess how long it took settlers to get from Independence, Missouri, to Fort Vancouver, Washington, a 2,000-mile journey by covered wagon along the Oregon Trail. Your child might be surprised to know that it took six months. Just for fun, try to imagine with your child what it would be like to move from one place to another today using a covered wagon as your moving van and home on wheels. Go from room to room, making lists of what you would take and what you would need to leave behind. Decide where your family is moving to and figure out its distance. Then calculate how long it will take to reach your new home traveling by covered wagon at a rate between ten to fifteen miles a day.

The Quest for Equality in America

Your child may be surprised to learn that women and African-Americans didn't have many rights until recently. When the Declaration of Independence was written in 1776, at least these civil liberties were denied to them:

* they weren't allowed to vote in elections
* they couldn't go to college
* women were limited in the jobs they could hold, while many African-Americans were held as slaves
* if a woman was married, all property belonged to her husband
* in the South, African-Americans did not have the legal right to marry

Emphasize that although problems still exist today, civil rights have improved greatly since that time, largely due to the efforts of social reformers. Have your child imagine a time travel scenario where a woman or African-American from the 1800s joins your family for dinner. What would he or she think of the roles of girls, boys, women, and men in your home? Talk about the power of using peaceful means to bring about change. Discuss news events that show progress of the continued need for change.

HISTORY ACTIVITIES

Famous Names

Even though the focus of social studies shouldn't be memorizing names and dates, your child does need to recognize important names. If someone is called a Benedict Arnold, is that a compliment or an insult? Play this family game to learn or practice names. Let each family member choose a different category—scientists, presidents, Native American leaders, suffragists, human rights advocates, villains, astronauts, and so on. Have each person write the names of 10 people on the front of index cards and an interesting fact about each on the back. Then cut the cards apart so the first names are separate from the last. Mix up the cards and together match, read, and sort them by category.

Time Lines

Encourage your child to research a topic that interests him or her, such as sports, the military, or flying machines. Have your child make a timeline to show how items relating to the topic changed over the years.

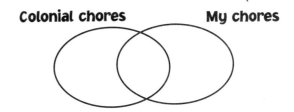

Draw Models

If you tell your child Columbus's ship the Santa Maria was about 75 to 90 feet long and had a crew of 40 men, he or she will probably say, "Oh." But if you go outside and measure and draw the boat, your child will begin to understand. Whenever possible draw models or make comparisons to help explain the numbers you are reading. For example, you could contrast the Santa Maria with the Queen Elizabeth 2, a modern ocean liner that is 963 feet long and has a crew of 900.

Then and Now

Let your child choose something from the past to compare with today, such as Washington and the current president or chores colonial children did and chores your child does. Have your child draw two overlapping ovals and label them. In the area that overlaps, direct your child to list similarities. In the remaining sections, have your child list differences.

Colonial chores   **My chores**

When I Was Your Age

To help your child better understand and appreciate differences—and similarities—between one generation and the next, describe what you remember about fourth grade. Include how people dressed and wore their hair, school procedures, major historical events that occurred, fads or favorite games, and items you didn't have that kids enjoy now. Share photo albums and scrap books, old home movies, clothing, or other items. If possible, involve grandparents and great-grandparents. You may want to videotape the family discussion for this generation's keepsake.

Art for Fourth Graders

Art and art appreciation have been integrated into nearly all curriculum areas, including language arts, mathematics, social studies, music, and even science. Fourth graders are aware that art is more than just drawing and coloring a picture. They are discovering the various forms of art—painting, sculpting, pottery, engraving, architecture. They are being introduced to elements of art—line, color, shape, texture. And they are beginning to explore different styles of art—folk art, Gothic art, pop art. The following ideas will help you explore art with your child.

WHAT'S ART?

The word art comes from the Latin *ars* which means "skill." What does art mean to your child? What does art mean to you? Share your ideas. Then together brainstorm a list of ways that people express themselves artistically. Ask your child to identify the ones which he or she enjoys or would like to explore. Here are some suggestions to get you started: painting, drawing, sculpting, carving, architecture, print making, decorative arts, photography.

BOOKS TO LOOK FOR

Here are some art books your child may enjoy:

Cathedral by David Macaulay (Houghton Mifflin, 1973)

Come Look With Me: Animals in Art by Gladys S. Blizzard (Thomasson-Grant, 1992) [series]

Georgia O'Keefe by Robyn Turner (Little, Brown, 1991) [series on women artists]

Lives of the Artists: Masterpieces, Messes (and What the Neighbors Thought) by Kathleen Krull (Harcourt Brace, 1995)

(Getting to Know the World's Greatest Artists) Picasso by Mike Venezia (Childrens, 1988) [series]

Talking With Artists: Volumes 1 and *2* edited by Pat Cummings (Bradbury, 1992)

ART ACTIVITIES

Cartoons and Comics

Have your child look through newspaper comic strips or study comic books to analyze how cartoonists show expression and movement. Ask questions such as these:

* Which characters look happy? surprised? mad? confused?
* How do the eyes help show emotion? How does the mouth? Are there other facial parts that give clues to a character's emotions?
* Which characters do you think are moving? What clues in the picture make you think that?

Afterwards, have your entire family try drawing actual cartoon characters or ones you invent. Remind your child that drawing takes practice. The more your child does it, the better he or she will get.

An Architectural Search

What are the buildings like in your community? Are they made from brick, wood, stucco, or marble? Do any public buildings or historic buildings have arches, domes, columns, or gargoyles? What shapes do they feature—rectangles, triangles, circles, semi-circles? Together go on a scavenger hunt and look for interesting architectural items. Have your child use page 91 to record observations. Your child may want to bring a camera to photograph buildings or features.

How Do You See It?

Look for examples of still-life paintings in art books, such as Vincent Van Gogh's *Sunflowers*. Ask your child to set up a still-life arrangement of a bowl of fruit, a vase of flowers, a group of toys, or any other objects he or she may want to use. Then have each family member draw or paint the still life as realistically as they can. Display the completed works of art to discuss, compare, and enjoy. On another occasion, have your child create a second still-life arrangement. This time challenge each family member to depict the arrangement as abstractly as possible. Compare the two styles and discuss which one each person prefers.

How Statuesque

Look around your home and community for examples of statues, sculptures, figurines, and so on. Talk about what they represent, the materials from which they were made, and how they may have been made. Then gather sculpting tools and either modeling clay, salt dough, or a bar of soap. Challenge your child to make a statue of a family pet, a friend, or a family member.

Visit an Art Museum

Take a family field trip to an art museum. Choose a topic to focus on or just explore on your own for fun. Be sure to stop by the gift shop at the end of the day and look for postcard prints, children's books, or activity kits.

Possible discussion topics:

How do artists use lines differently?

What shapes do you see?

What is your eye most drawn to in each piece?

How does the title refer to the piece?

What patterns can you find?

How do colors affect the mood of the artwork?

Music for Fourth Graders

Music and music appreciation, just like the visual arts, have been integrated into many curriculum areas. Fourth graders should be familiar with some of the basic elements of music—rhythm and melody—that composers use to create a piece. They should also be able to recognize different styles of music and families of musical instruments. Use the following ideas to build on your child's knowledge.

NAME THAT TUNE!

Help your child develop a greater understanding and appreciation for classical music by playing a variation of the old television quiz show "Name That Tune." First encourage your child to share his or her knowledge of classical music with you. Here are some concepts you may want to supplement:

* Classical music includes symphonies, chamber music, ballet music, operas, and oratorios.
* It is generally more complicated than other kinds of music.

* It is performed by highly-skilled and well-trained musicians.

Next listen to some of the more well-known composers and their works, such as Vivaldi's *The Four Seasons*, Handel's *Water Music* or *The Messiah*, Beethoven's *Fifth Symphony* or *Ninth Symphony "Choral,"* Tchaikovsky's *Nutcracker Suite*, Bach's *Brandenburg Concertos*, Pachelbel's *Canon*, and Mozart's *Jupiter Symphony* or *Requiem*. Take your child to live performances if possible. Listen to a local classical radio station.

Before long, your child will be humming a symphony.

For the game "Name That Tune," simply play short excerpts from the various works you've listen to previously to see if your child can identify them. Try a similar approach to introduce music from other cultures.

BOOKS TO LOOK FOR

American Indian Music and Musical Instruments by George S. Fitcher (McKay, 1978)

Her Piano Sang—A Story about Clara Schumann by Barbara Allman (Carolrhoda, 1997) (Creative Minds series)

Music by Neil Ardley (Knopf, 1989) (Eyewitness Books series)

Sing Me a Story—The Metropolitan Opera's® Book of Opera Stories for Children by Jane Rosenberg (Thames and Hudson, 1989)

Ben Franklin's Glass Armonica by Priscilla Kiedrowski (Carolrhoda, 1983)

The Golden Song Book by Katherine Tyler Wessells (Western, 1981)

MUSIC NOTATION AND TERMS

Notes and Rests

Here are some note and rest symbols your child should know or learn. If these are new to your family, you may want to look for examples of these notes and rests in songbooks.

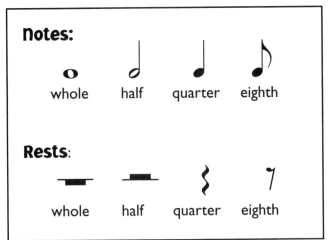

It's About Time

A time signature, found at the beginning of a piece of music, is an example of how math and music are related.

The top number tells how many beats there are in each measure (the unit from one bar to the next). The bottom number tells which note equals one beat. For example, a time signature of $\frac{4}{4}$ means there are four beats in each measure and a quarter note gets one beat. In $\frac{3}{4}$ time, there are three beats in each measure and a quarter note gets one beat.

Some types of music are known for their time signature. You may want to listen to a waltz by Johann Strauss and see if you can recognize the $\frac{3}{4}$ time. You may even want to dance along (1, 2, 3, 1, 2, 3 . . .)

Would You Repeat That Please?

Tap or clap out some rhythms such as these:

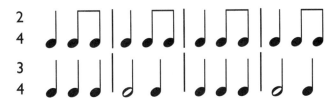

Challenge your child to repeat the rhythm patterns after you. Then have your child make his or her own rhythm patterns for you to listen to and repeat. Try writing the rhythm patterns you make up.

CDE or Do Re Mi

Show the following C major scale to your child, or play it on a piano, synthesizer, or other musical instrument, if available:

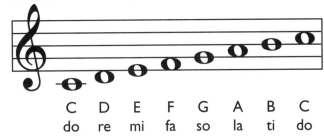

Teach your child that the notes of the C major scale are sometimes called by sounds instead of letter names. Have your child sing the sound names going up the scale—do, re, mi, fa, so, la, ti, do—and back down, again—do, ti, la, so, fa, mi, re, do. Use the song "Do-Re-Mi" from *The Sound of Music* to help your child learn the scale. For fun, challenge your child to use the sound names in place of words to sing familiar childhood songs such as "Row, Row, Row Your Boat," "Frere Jacques," and "Twinkle, Twinkle, Little Star." Use page 92 to get started.

MORE MUSIC FUN

Musical Pictures

Play a recording of *The Grand Canyon Suite* by Ferde Grofé, an American composer who created musical portraits of some of America's natural wonders. As your child listens to the movements, ask how he or she visualizes the "Sunrise" and "The Painted Desert," riding a donkey "On the Trail," the "Sunset," and getting caught in a "Cloudburst." Your child may enjoy drawing or painting what he or she "sees" on this musical journey through the Grand Canyon.

Creating a Mood

Have your child analyze the music of a TV program, movie, or video. Direct your child to view, listen, and take notes about the connection between the music and the characters and events. Your child may want to look away and just listen. Can he or she tell by the music when something bad will happen? something silly? Were there times when the music overpowered the visuals? Talk about what your child discovered.

We've Got Rhythm

Invite your child to help you gather the "instruments" to make a family rhythm band. You can tap empty milk jugs and different-size plastic soda bottles. You can strum an old washboard with a sewing thimble. You can "play" two tablespoons by placing the handles between the first and middle fingers and the middle and third fingers so the rounded bowls touch lightly. By holding the spoons loosely and slapping them together in the palm of your other hand or between your knee and hand, you can click out a rhythm. You can also "play" a tin can, a cake pan, a pail, a flower pot, an old hubcap, and a pot by tapping out a rhythm with a pencil or spoon. Experiment with the various "instruments" and the many sounds and the rhythms you can create.

It's Instrumental

How many instruments can you name? Have a contest between family members to see who can write the longest list. Let your child look in books to supplement the list if he or she wants. Then read the lists aloud. Have family members talk about which instruments they have seen, heard, or played. You may also want to categorize the instruments as strings, brass, woodwinds, or percussion.

A Family Sing Along

Encourage your family to sing together—whether it's Beatles songs, musicals, rounds, religious music, folk music, or the blues. Choose a style everyone likes or take turns choosing the theme of songs for that night. Some children who struggle reading books have much more confidence reading lyrics to a song they are familiar with. If you don't have a selection of music at home, check the music section at your library.

FS-23005 Skills for Success for Your Fourth Grader • © Frank Schaffer Publications, Inc.

Physical Education for Fourth Graders

Physical education is an important part of the total school curriculum. It provides children with the opportunities they need to develop and improve basic motor skills like running, throwing, and jumping. As children participate in specific kinds of activities, they increase their strength, flexibility, and endurance, thus developing their physical fitness. A physical education program also enables children to develop the knowledge and attitudes they need to participate in physical activities and sports. Fourth graders learn the skills needed to participate in many popular sports and activities, such as basketball, soccer, softball, touch football, volleyball, gymnastics, and track-and-field. They also learn the rules and play actual games.

FAMILY FUN

Make physical activity a family event. If possible, set aside a specific day and time to exercise as a family. Take turns choosing the activity. Try something new. Take a family lesson. Involve friends or neighbors if you need more people to play a game. Ideas:

* hike
* swim
* bike
* jog
* ice skate
* roller skate
* bowl
* skateboard
* sail
* dive
* surf
* ski
* snowboard
* sled
* dance
* wrestle
* do gymnastics
* do aerobics
* do karate
* do archery
* go horseback riding
* play soccer
* play basketball
* play volleyball
* play baseball
* play football
* play kickball
* play street hockey
* play field hockey
* play ice hockey
* play tag

OFF TO A GOOD START

There are some who think that children are naturally active and in shape, but that's not so. Children need to get exercise four or five times a week, and many just do not. You can help your child by establishing good health habits early. Here are four suggestions to consider:

1. Do something active with your child when you are spending time together. Make a list of some possible activities that you both might enjoy doing together.

2. Exercise regularly yourself to set a positive example.

3. Encourage your child to ride a bike or walk whenever possible and to take the stairs instead of the elevator.

4. Think about limiting the amount of time your child spends watching TV. It's one reason why children don't exercise enough.

SPORTS AND FITNESS

Are You Ready?

Ceiling Stretch—Stand and reach up to the ceiling.

Floor Stretch—Stand and reach down to the floor.

Side Stretch—Stand and hold your left arm over your head. Bend to the right side. Repeat with your right arm raised and bend to the left.

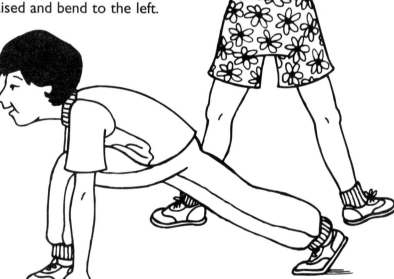

Over the Shoulder Stretch—Stand or sit. Raise your right arm and place your right hand over your shoulder and behind your back. Try to touch or grasp it with your left hand. Repeat with opposite arms.

Leg Stretch—Squat with your left leg bent and your right leg straight behind you. Your bent knee should line up with your ankle. Stretch and hold, using your hands for support. Switch legs and repeat.

FAMILY FITNESS FUN

Family Sports Festival

Make up your own family sports festival. Choose ten events, such as a basketball toss, 100 meter dash, long jump, 50 meter three-legged race, criss-cross jump roping, and an obstacle course. Adjust heights and distances to make it more fair for younger family members. Involve everyone in measuring and timekeeping. Let individuals or teams compete at least twice in each event so that you can track improvement. Give out awards for Best Sport, Best Improved, Most Likely to Enter the Olympics, and so on.

Let's Dance!

Dance and movement most likely are an important part of your child's P.E. program at school. Follow up with some dancing at home. Invite your child to teach you a line dance or square dance he or she has learned. Then teach the family some dances you know.

Go to a Game

Watching high school players, college athletes, or professionals can be very motivating for children. If you can, go early and watch the players warm up. Or stay later and let your child try to speak with an athlete after a game or meet. College athletes may be more willing to do this than professionals.

A Personal Pledge

Discuss the importance of physical fitness with your child. Then together brainstorm some of the things you and your child can do to stay healthy and fit. Here are some possibilities:

* set exercise goals that are realistic and keep them
* exercise on a regular basis for at least 20 minutes three times a week
* warm up before exercising, cool down after exercising
* walk or ride a bike whenever you can, instead of riding in a car or bus

Then have your child write and sign a pledge to keep fit.

Reluctant Athletes

When you were a kid, were you the first one picked to play shortstop or the last one picked and sent to the outfield? If children aren't "good," they get picked last, stuck where they'll do the least harm, and rarely get better because they're not doing anything. If your child is unhappy about being in this position, you can help. Great baseball players are great because they play all the time. Take time to teach and practice the skills needed to play a game—throwing, catching, batting, and so on. You can begin easy, tossing a ball or beanbag a short distance back and forth, and then progress to harder skills. If you never learned these basics, either learn together or get a friend, relative, or neighbor to help your child.

Social Skills

In addition to academics, your child needs social skills to succeed at school, at home, with friends, and in the community. This next section contains information and activities to help you with your child's social skills.

R-E-S-P-E-C-T

Respect is at the core of our interactions with others. It is showing regard or consideration for people and things. Hold a family discussion and talk about ways family members treat each other with respect. Almost any situation can be thought of in terms of respect or a lack of respect. Here are some family situations you might want to talk about. If they show a lack of respect, how could the family member do something differently to be more respectful?

* saying hello to guests when they come over
* interrupting someone who is trying to talk
* asking if you can borrow something from a sibling
* slamming your door
* taking care of library books
* calling home if you are going to be late
* introducing your family to your friends

If your family has problems showing respect toward one another, you may want to set aside a week for everyone to focus on respect. Begin by naming ways parents can show respect so that children don't think it's only kids who need to be respectful.

RESPECT AT SCHOOL

Discuss different ways a child can show concern, appreciation, and consideration, (or in other words respect) for others in the school setting. Ask your child to think about how he or she would answer each of these questions. Include any others that come to mind.

* Are you sometimes mean or unfriendly to others because they look different from you?

* Do you sometimes laugh at children who may not be as smart as you?
* Do you sometimes talk back to your teachers?
* Do you ever forget to say *please* and *thank you*?
* Do you ever talk when others are trying to talk?
* Do you ever make fun of other children's ideas or beliefs because they're not the same as yours?

Explain that a yes answer to any of the questions means your child may have some work to do when it comes to showing respect for others. Encourage your child to make a pledge to be respectful of others. Remind your child that treating others the way he or she would like to be treated can be a good way to begin.

TAKE RESPONSIBILITY

Invent a character, such as Blamer. Invite family members to make up stories about how Blamer never takes personal responsibility for his or her actions, but instead blames it on others. Then whenever family members forget to take responsibility for their actions, everyone can give them this friendly reminder, "Don't be like Blamer!"

At Home and At School

What are you responsible for at home? What is your child responsible for? Have each family member make a list of their personal responsibilities at home. If anyone's list is excessively long or way too short, you may want to redivide responsibilities. Next have your child list his or her responsibilities at school and the teacher's responsibilities. It is important for children to realize that in order for a family, a class, or a community to thrive, everyone must live up to their responsibilities.

Oh No, I Forgot My Homework!

Does your child ever forget his or her homework? Does it happen frequently? Help your child make a checklist of "Things to Do Before Bedtime." Be sure to include putting homework in the backpack or book bag. Then just before bedtime, encourage your child to review the checklist. What should your child tell the teacher if he or she happens to forget anyway? The truth. Encourage your child to own up to it, face the consequences, and then bring the homework to school the next day. This can also help to dispel any thoughts the teacher might have had that your child hadn't completed the assignment in the first place.

Lying

No matter how bad an act it is, most parents would rather hear the truth than have a child lie about it. Let your child know that. Take the opportunity to discuss why lying is not a good way to handle a problem. Point out that lies are usually discovered and that when they are, you get in trouble for lying and for what you lied about. The worst part about lying is that others may doubt you in future situations when you are telling the truth. Explain that getting away with a lie can be just as bad because you are in trouble with yourself. A guilty conscience can be a very uncomfortable feeling.

MANNERS

Please, Thank You, You're Welcome, Excuse Me

Children are taught these four phrases beginning at age one. Yet we can all name some children and adults who still do not use these simple courtesies. When you see or hear a situation in your home where someone could have been more courteous, be sure to gently point it out to the offender. Modeling polite behavior and having your child model it for his or her peers is a powerful way to teach courtesy.

Manners Matter

As you will more than likely agree, manners are very important, even in school. Ask your child to give you some examples of manners that are appropriate in various school settings. Jot down your child's suggestions. Here are a few to help your child get started:

1. Say *please* when you ask for something.

2. Say *thank you* when someone gives you something or helps you.

3. Introduce your friends to others who may not know them.

4. Say, "It's nice to meet you," or something similar, when introduced to someone new.

5. Speak courteously to peers and adults.

6. When eating, take small bites and chew with your mouth closed.

7. Don't talk when you have a mouthful of food.

8. Use a napkin, not your hand or sleeve, to wipe your mouth.

9. Hold the door for the person behind you.

10. Offer to help if you see someone who needs it.

At a Friend's Home

Summer is a great time to play with friends. It's also a great time for a refresher discussion on how to act when going over to a friend's home. You can ask questions like these:

✷ How can you be polite to your friend's parents?
(Say hello when you walk in; Look them in the eye when speaking; Ask, don't tell; Be courteous.)

✷ How can you be polite to your friend?
(Take turns; Offer to help clean up messes you both made.)

✷ How can you be polite to your friend's younger brothers or sisters?
(Don't call them names; Don't take things without asking.)

✷ How can you be polite to your friend's older brothers or sisters?
(Don't enter their room without permission; Invite them to join you if they are close in age.)

FRIENDSHIP

Where to Play?

Playing with friends is often a child's favorite part of the day. Fourth graders usually don't need parents to referee as younger kids do. But they still need to have a parent nearby in case they get into mischief or need help. Encourage your child to balance his or her play at your home and at the homes of friends. Some children are shy about going to other children's homes. If your child is reluctant to leave, you may want to visit friends where both the kids and the parents get along so you can be there. If your child is always at a friend's home, try to have the kids play at your home, too. This will help you get to know your child's friends and see how they interact.

No One Likes Me

Does your child have a problem making or keeping friends in school? Talk about it together. Ask your child what the problem might be. Encourage your child to think about his or her own behavior and attitudes. You may want to suggest these questions:

Am I too bossy?
Am I too competitive?
Am I a bad loser?
Do I boast every time I win?
Do I give other kids a chance to talk or do I hog the conversation?
Do I listen to what others are saying?
Do I act like a show-off or a know-it-all?
Do kids think I'm a snob because I'm so shy?

Next, ask your child to think about some of the children he or she admires and how they make and keep friends. What are the qualities that he or she admires in them? Then encourage your child to identify his or her own best qualities. Jot them down. Together determine whether your child is applying any of these good qualities and skills. Do some role playing so your child can practice and experiment with the skills he or she needs to interact better with peers. Offer possible strategies to try. As your child begins to feel more comfortable and confident, encourage opportunities to practice, such as inviting a friend to go to the movies or to come over to play. Try not to push too hard.

Making New Friends

You may want to check into different community organizations such as the scouts, the Y, and religious groups, where your child can meet other children with similar interests. As your child tries to make new friends, provide feedback. Offer praise as new skills are learned and applied and possible alternatives when something doesn't work. It's also important to remember that to feel accepted, a person really needs only one or two good friends.

SCHOOL RULES

What Are the Rules?

Find out the rules your child is expected to follow and then discuss them together. Emphasize that school rules are established to help maintain the health, safety, and well being of everyone—students, teachers, aides, office staff, custodial staff, cafeteria workers, and so on. Rules also let children know exactly what kinds of behavior are not acceptable.

If your child complains that certain rules are "dumb" or "stupid" or "unfair," find out why. Creating "what if" situations may help your child to better understand the purpose of a certain rule or the consequences of not following it. For example, what if a child decides to punch or trip a classmate? What rules are broken? What are the consequences for the children involved? How should someone treat a person that he or she doesn't like? Why? And what should your child do if he or she is ever punched or tripped? Should he or she punch back, get the help of a teacher, do nothing? What does your child think? What do you think? What rules does the school have that address such a situation?

What If You Don't Agree With a Rule?

Should you happen to strongly disagree with a certain rule, perhaps because it conflicts with a rule you have at home, talk it over with your child's teacher or the school administrator. Keep in mind, however, that your child may be expected to follow certain rules no matter what.

Just as your child is expected to follow certain rules of conduct at home, in the family car, at the homes of friends and relatives, and in public places, your child is also expected to follow certain rules of conduct at school.

In an Emergency

Point out to your child that there may be situations in which rules can be broken without fear of the consequences. For example, should your child see someone who is badly hurt, he or she may decide to run to the office or shout for help, thereby disobeying the rules for no running or shouting in the hallway. Talk about how to make decisions in such situations and the importance of using good judgment.

CLASSROOM ISSUES

I Forgot My Lunch Money

How often does your child forget to bring lunch money to school? Solve the problem by giving your child lunch money the night before and suggesting that he or she put it in the book bag or backpack or in the pocket of tomorrow's outfit. You might also want to give your child "emergency money" to keep in a binder or a hidden pocket of a jacket or book bag.

Discuss possible options in the event your child forgets his or her lunch or lunch money anyway. Should your child inform the teacher? Does the cafeteria have a charge system? Is there someone at home to call who can bring the lunch or money to school? Children need to eat in order to work effectively in the afternoon. Let your child know that he or she should not get upset, stay quiet, and go hungry.

But I Didn't Do It . . .

Being blamed for something you didn't do can be upsetting at any age. Should this happen to your child at school, suggest that he or she speak up—politely, of course. Talk about possible things to say. For example, your child might say, "I wouldn't do something like that. What makes you think I did it?" If your child is too mad or upset to speak about it, suggest he or she write a letter to the person.

I Don't Feel Well!

You've probably filled out an emergency card for your child with medical information, people to be called, and so on. But make sure your child knows what to do in case of illness—tell the teacher, see the school nurse, call you, and so on. If you notice any symptoms of illness in the morning, perhaps your child should stay home for the day, not only so that he or she can fight the illness but to prevent spreading it to others.

Test Time

Fourth grade is often a transition year when school work becomes more difficult and testing more commonplace. Some children get nervous or even sick before a test. If your child is anxious, try to reassure him or her that the results—terrific, fair, poor, or otherwise—will not change who your child is or your feelings for him or her. Help your child study by giving a practice test. Praise your child if he or she does know the information and give words of encouragement for the upcoming test. Afterwards talk about the test and how your child felt about it. If your child was disappointed about the score, suggest he or she begin studying sooner for the next one.

SPEAKING UP

Speaking in Front of a Group

Try to remember what it was like to have to stand up in front of the class to give an oral report, to introduce yourself to people you didn't know, to ask a question when you didn't understand something, to be called on to answer a question, or to appear before your parents and your friends' parents in a play. For some children, the very thought of speaking in such situations causes fear and panic.

There are some things you can do to help your child become more comfortable when speaking in front of others. Begin by having your child make a list of the situations that cause the most anxiety and fear and then rate them in some way. For example, asking a question in class may cause only mild fear, while giving a speech in front of parents may cause overwhelming anxiety.

Help your child work on each of the situations, one by one, through a series of practice sessions. Make the sessions short at first. If your child has to give a book report, suggest that he or she read the report in front of a mirror. When your child begins to feel more confident, have him or her read the book report to you. Next time, increase the audience by including other family members or friends. Encourage your child to relax and to counter negative thoughts with positive ones. For example, if your child is thinking "My throat is so dry I can't speak," suggest that he or she say something like this instead "I can speak, no matter how dry my mouth gets."

I'm Afraid to Ask Questions

Some children are afraid to ask questions in class. They think the teacher will get mad or other children will laugh at them. If your child complains that these events have actually occurred, you may want to speak with the teacher. If the fears are just imagined, give your child experience asking questions at home and in other situations.

1. Encourage discussions at dinnertime in which family members ask one another questions about the events of the day. For fun, you might challenge each family member to come up with the silliest (dumbest, craziest) question. The winner might get an extra cookie! The idea is to foster a relaxed atmosphere in which communication can occur, free of fear.

2. Let your child ask about something when you are at the library, a store, or other public place. For example, if your child wants to know where a drinking fountain is or where to find a book, have him or her ask the question, not you.

PROBLEMS WITH PEERS

Give Me Your Lunch Money or Else

Does your child know what to do if he or she has become the target of the class bully? It's important to remember these points:

* the bully usually "hits" when adults of authority are out of sight
* victims often say nothing out of fear
* frequent victimization can destroy a child's confidence, making it difficult to cope
* bullying doesn't just go away on its own
* a child can't always handle bullying on his or her own

If your child is the target of a bully, talk about how to act and what to do when it happens. Try doing some role playing so your child can practice possible responses. Because your child may be too afraid to report incidents of bullying, it is up to you to tell the teacher. You'll also have to do some damage control like reassuring your child that he or she *is* special, bright, strong, etc. to help restore your child's confidence.

Should I Tell on My Friend?

Your child may observe a friend doing something wrong at school, such as lying to the teacher, stealing a classmate's money, cheating on a test, or copying homework. What should your child do? If your child tells, he or she may lose a friend. If your child remains silent, how will that affect his or her own feelings and conscience? Suppose the teacher asks, for example, "Who stole Angela's money?" Should your child blurt out the friend's name or tell the teacher in private? Probably not. Encourage your child to persuade the "culprit" to do the right thing.

Psst . . . Let Me See Your Answers

"Keep your eyes on your own paper" are the words frequently uttered by teachers during tests. Your child undoubtedly knows that cheating is wrong, but is he or she comfortable saying no to such a request from a best friend and then covering up the answers? If not, he or she should be. Remind your child that letting a friend copy test answers is also cheating and that real friends should not expect each other to cheat. Suggest that your child have the friend come over and study together so they are both ready for the next test.

Home and School Cooperation

GETTING ORGANIZED

If you have a child who is consistently disorganized, try to find ways to prove that being organized really does make life easier. Setting goals and priorities, planning ahead, budgeting time wisely, keeping track of assignments, and gathering the materials needed to complete assignments are just a few of the skills that will help your child to be a good student. If you are met with resistance, suggest some work-together situations where you teach or model how to get organized. Involve your child in the planning. When you begin, make sure your child understands just what the goal is each time—to organize a notebook or backpack; to organize a desk or closet; to organize a pack of baseball cards or toys and games; to complete a science project, history report, or book report.

> Where's my backpack? I can't find my science book. I don't have a pencil or a pen. I left my homework on the table and now it's gone. These are the words of a child who may need some help getting organized.

A STEP-BY-STEP PLAN

Does the thought of cleaning his or her bedroom or writing a report overwhelm your child? Teach your child how to write a step-by-step plan. First list all the things that need to get done that relate to the project. Next label each item *F* for first, *M* for middle, or *L* for last depending on when it needs to or could be done.

Then go back and number the steps, starting with all the firsts, then the middles, and ending with all the lasts. As your child completes each step, have him or her cross it off. By breaking up a large project into smaller tasks, your child can get going and feel a sense of accomplishment.

Cleaning My Room

F	2	pick up dirty clothes
M	5	put away clean clothes
M	7	throw away/recycle papers and junk
M	4	put away toys and games
L	8	vacuum
L	9	dust
F	3	put away books
M	6	clean off top of desk
F	1	make bed

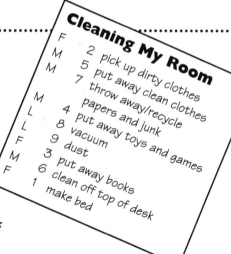

COMMUNICATION

A Checklist of Things to Do

Are your mornings spent searching for the sweater your child wanted to wear? Do you ever get a phone call asking that the forgotten lunch or homework be brought to school? Is your child periodically tardy? Some children and some families just aren't morning people. Suggest creating a checklist of things to do each night before going to bed so that the morning rush becomes less chaotic and more productive.

Checklist
- ☐ homework
- ☐ lunch or lunch money
- ☐ signed notes
- ☐ clothes for tomorrow
- ☐ backpack ready

As you provide different opportunities for your child to practice and apply organizational skills and techniques, talk about how they helped to make tasks easier. Encourage your child to practice these newly acquired organizational skills every day so that they become an automatic part of his or her routine. Above all, try to be patient and supportive and to acknowledge your child's efforts and progress.

Let's Talk

Parent: What did you do in school today?
Child: Nothing.

If your after-school conversations are similar to the one above, you may want to try a different approach. First, let your child have a snack and relax. Then try one of these conversation starters:

✳ What was the best thing that happened today?
✳ What was the worst thing that happened today?
✳ What did your class do during music today?
✳ What are those things hanging from the ceiling in your classroom?
✳ The newsletter said your class's play will be next Friday night. How are rehearsals going?

A Daily Checklist From School

If your child has a consistent problem with behavior, finishing schoolwork, transporting assignments and notes to and from school, or another school situation, see if the teacher would be willing to provide daily feedback in the form of a checklist. Offer to create and provide the checklist forms, with input from your child and the teacher. You may want to create a form your child completes and the teacher signs off on. Set up a simple reward system at home if the daily reports are positive.

PARENT-TEACHER CONFERENCES

Effective communication between you and your child's teacher is essential. Most schools have structured conferences two or three times a year. In addition, you can always send a note to the teacher requesting a mini-conference before or after school, or on the phone. Here are some things you may want to consider as you prepare for a conference:

Schoolwork—What is the quality of your child's work that has come home? Is your child completing assignments?

Attitude—Does your child want to go to school in the morning? Is he or she an eager participant or a reluctant participant at school?

Peers—How does your child get along with others in the class? on the playground? at home?

Home life—Is anything major going on at home that could affect your child's behavior or schoolwork—birth of a sibling, loss of a job, divorce, a death or illness in the family, the death of a pet? [Although this family information is private, you may want to share it with the teacher so he or she can keep you abreast of how it may be affecting your child at school.]

Many teachers send home a questionnaire before the conference. If your child's teacher does not, jot down specific questions you have.

As the teacher discusses your child, listen carefully to what he or she has to say. If you find yourself wanting to argue or disagree, try to wait until he or she has finished. Then ask questions related to the comments and request specifics: "You mentioned that my child has trouble paying attention. What does she do? Does it happen all the time?" Ask your child's teacher if there is anything you can do to help.

Remember that your child's teacher has many parents to see, so watch the time. If necessary, set up another conference for the near future.

WELCOME TO OPEN HOUSE

Open House is often the first major event of the school year. It gives you an opportunity to see your child's classroom, to hear what plans your child's teacher has for the year, to get acquainted with the school program, and to examine your child's work to date. It is important to remember that an open house is not the time to talk about specific problems or your concerns with the teacher. Save them for a parent-teacher conference.

HOMEWORK

Some Words of Advice

1. Make sure your child has a quiet place to do homework—a desk, the kitchen table, a chair or bed for reading. Is there adequate lighting? Does your child have the appropriate materials to complete the assignments? Can they be stored together at a desk or in a supplies box?

Work Supplies

- lined writing paper
- graph paper
- construction paper
- sharpened pencils
- pens
- highlighter
- colored pencils, crayons, or markers
- erasers
- scissors
- ruler (inches/centimeters)
- tape
- glue
- calculator
- dictionary
- thesaurus
- globe or world map
- U.S. map

2. Work out a set of rules together, such as no lengthy telephone calls or television while doing homework. Listening to music is another matter, as many children work well with background music. If it helps, leave it on. If the music is distracting, turn it off.

3. Have your child set a regular schedule for homework time that fits with his or her other activities. Many kids need time to eat and relax after school. Just make it clear to your child that you expect the homework to be completed and that it is his or her responsibility to do it.

> If homework is a hassle in your household, there are some practical things you can do to help alleviate the pressure.

4. If you are asked for help, try not to fall into the trap of doing your child's homework. You can help by listening to spelling or vocabulary words or by asking questions if your child is preparing for a test. If your child doesn't understand an assignment, try to explain it by making up a few examples of your own.

5. If a note needs to be written telling why homework was not finished, have your child write and sign it. You can then sign it, too.

A Homework Contract

You may want to have a homework contract, like that on page 94, between you and your child. For example, your child may agree to complete assignments on time, check all homework, and read every night for 20 minutes, while you may agree to provide a quiet place to study and to be willing to answer questions or check over certain assignments. Positive consequences may include computer game privileges or a special family outing. Negative consequences may include losing TV privileges or playtime with friends if homework is not completed.

VOLUNTEERING

Schools need parental support. The more you can give, the better for your child and all the children at school. Volunteering also offers benefits for parents. Here is a list of some benefits you can gain by being a school volunteer.

1. You know what is going on at school.
2. You meet teachers, the principal, and other staff.
3. Your child's teacher sees you more frequently and can let you know if anything is up.
4. You get to meet your child's classmates and see how they interact.
5. Your child knows you care about school.

At School—If you have time during the day, you may want to volunteer in your child's classroom or another part of the school. Here are some activities you could be asked to do:

* check attendance
* duplicate worksheets
* gather supplies
* distribute materials
* record information
* file children's papers
* maintain classroom library
* operate audio-visual equipment
* deliver messages
* play learning games with children
* read to or listen to small groups or individual children
* help during field trips

At Home—If you work (including caring for young children) and can't get time off during the day, you can still volunteer. Here are a few things you can do at home:

* schedule speakers or field trips
* gather materials for special projects
* make telephone calls for the teacher
* make games and flashcards
* type
* translate forms or stories
* proofread teacher-created materials, class books, and class newspapers
* make costumes

Your child's teacher will appreciate any time you can give whether it's once during the year or every week.

LIMITING TV TIME

Most children enjoy watching television. It's a way to relax and it gives them something to talk about with their friends. Unfortunately, many children watch too much television. When it interferes with homework, family relationships, and getting enough exercise, you have a problem. Here are some tips:

* Set a time limit.
* If school work is suffering, consider restricting TV during the week to one program a day.
* Be aware of what your child is watching.
* Watch and discuss programs as a family.
* Provide family alternatives to watching TV—games, reading, music, exercise.

Bookmarks

NO MATTER how you **measure** it,  **YOU** are measuring **UP!**

Keep on going! **You'll MAKE it!**

Just a few notes to say **A GREAT PERFORMANCE!**

I SPY A Shining STAR!

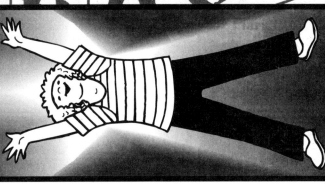

EXTRA!!! EXTRA!!! *Read all about it!*  does a **GREAT** job!

Backs of Bookmarks

 FS-23005 Skills for Success for Your Fourth Grader • © Frank Schaffer Publications, Inc.

Similarities and Differences

Compare yourself to a child character in a novel you've read.
First draw and label a picture of each of you. Then fill in the chart.

Me

Character

We are similar in these ways:

1. _____

2. _____

3. _____

We are different in these ways:

1. _____

2. _____

3. _____

1. _____

2. _____

3. _____

Watch for Signs

Here are some common signs that use symbols instead of words. Mark a ✔ next to each one you can find. Write where you saw it and what you think it means.

Sign	✔	Location found/ Sign's meaning	Sign	✔	Location found/ Sign's meaning
(deer crossing symbol)			(picnic table symbol)		
(no bicycles symbol)			(wheelchair accessible symbol)		
DO NOT ENTER			(slippery road symbol)		
(no smoking symbol)			(telephone symbol)		
(no left turn symbol)			(pedestrian crossing symbol)		
(pedestrian crossing symbol)			(skull and crossbones symbol)		
(first aid cross symbol)			(train XING symbol)		

Bonus! Design a sign for your room, the kitchen, or another room in your home.

Dots and Letters

People who are blind can read using Braille. They run their fingers over groups of raised dots. Each group stands for a different letter. The Braille system was invented by Louis Braille. He was born in France. He lost his sight when he was just three years old. Here is the Braille alphabet. The letters are made by arranging up to six dots. If you want to feel them, poke a tiny hole with a straight pin from underneath the paper.

 The Braille cell is three dots high and two dots wide. This means that you can form up to 63 characters.

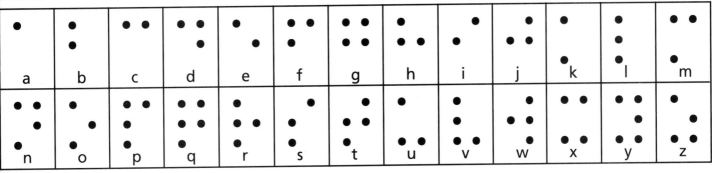

Decode this Braille message to learn more about the inventor of Braille.

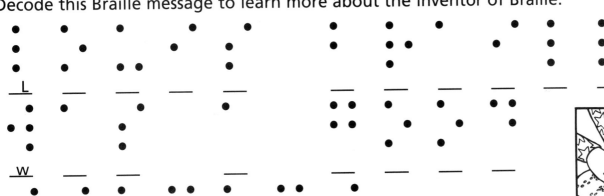

L _ _ _ _ _ _ _ _ _ _

W _ _ _ _ _

s _ _ _ .

Write a message using the Braille alphabet. Give it to someone in your family to read.

The 5 W's

The 5 W's tell the most important facts in a news story—who, what, where, when, and why. Choose a newspaper story to read. Then complete this form. Use your notes to tell your family about the story.

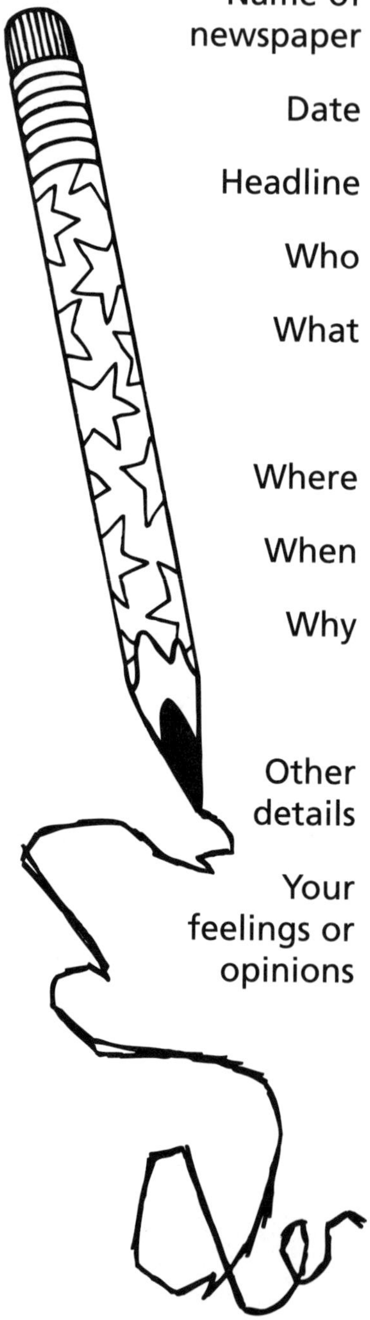

Name of
newspaper _____

Date _____

Headline _____

Who _____

What _____

_____

Where _____

When _____

Why _____

_____

Other
details _____

Your
feelings or
opinions _____

_____

_____

Don't Be Confused!

These word pairs are homophones—words that sound alike, but have different spellings and meanings. Fill in each sentence with the correct pair of words. Check in a dictionary if you are not sure what a word means.

through	who's	forth	you're	weave
threw	whose	fourth	your	we've
piece	past	weather	plain	heel
peace	passed	whether	plane	heal
whole	clothes	where	principle	
hole	close	wear	principal	

1. If _____ careful, _____ plan is sure to succeed.

2. _____ going to tell me _____ jacket this is?

3. My brother accidentally _____ the baseball _____ the window.

4. To keep the _____, we gave each child a small _____.

5. Our school _____ gave a speech about the _____ of free speech.

6. On the _____ of the month, we will go _____ with our plans.

7. Who cares _____ it's cloudy and cold; bad _____ never stopped us before.

8. It took a month for the bruise on my _____ to _____.

9. _____ been learning how to _____ cloth from wool.

10. It's _____ to see that the pilot had no choice but to land the _____ in the field.

11. It's hard to believe that a small _____ could have caused the _____ thing to be ruined.

12. I'm supposed to _____ boots in case it rains, but I don't know _____ they are.

13. You'll never _____ that suitcase with all those _____ in it!

14. Don't you think this _____ year _____ by quickly?

Step by Step

Worksheet

Write step-by-step directions for making or doing something.

Directions for ______________________________

You will need these materials:

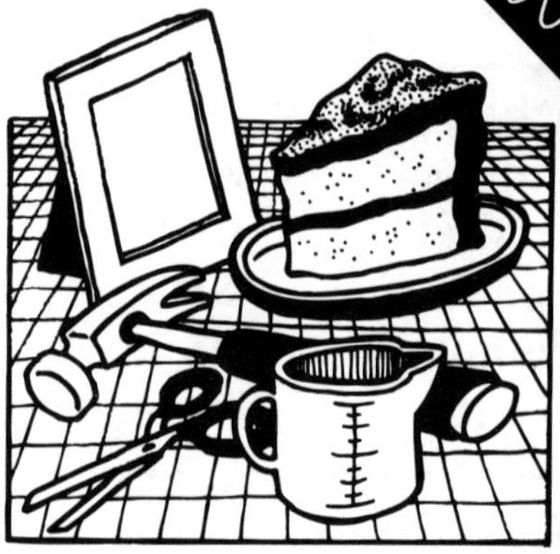

____

____

____

____

Here's What to Do:

Some Diagrams to Help You:

1 ______________________________

____

____

2 ______________________________

____

____

3 ______________________________

____

____

4 ______________________________

____

____

Organize a Scary Story

Worksheet

Answer these questions to help plan a scary story. Then write your story.

Setting

Where does your story take place? ______________________________

____

When does it take place? ______________________________

____

Characters

Who are the main characters? What are they like?

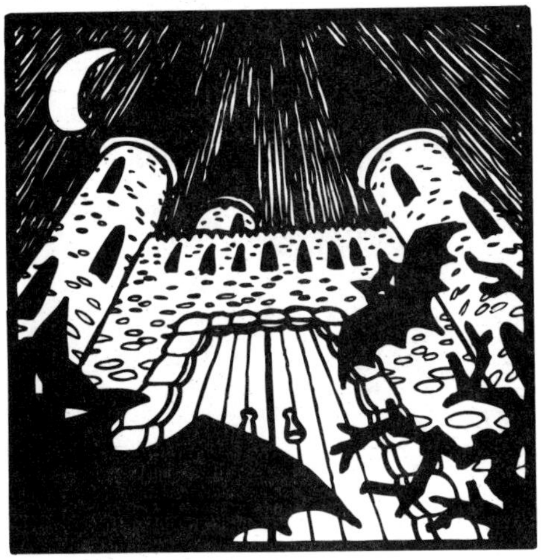

____

____

____

Plot

What happens in the story? What is the main problem to be solved?

____

____

____

What is the climax? (the most dramatic point)

____

What is the conclusion? ______________________________

____

Title

What is the title? ______________________________

Follow the Signs

See how quickly you can get to the end of the path.
Follow the signs to do the math.
Hint! The answers in the triangular-shaped stones should all be the same.

$0 + 8 = \times 2 = + 4 =$ △ $\div 5 = \times 9 + 7 = - 23 = $ △ $+ 20 = - 4 = \div 6 = \times 8 = $ △ $+ 1 = 80 - = 52 + = \div 3 = \times 4 = - 8 = $ △

Just the Facts!

Complete this multiplication table.

Time: _____ minutes
Score: _____

X	0	1	2	3	4	5	6	7	8	9
0										
1										
2										
3			6							
4										
5										
6										
7										
8										
9										

What's the Volume?

Measure four box-shaped objects around your home. Then calculate the volume of each object by multiplying its length x width x height. Your answer should be in cubic inches or cubic centimeters.

Object: Cereal box

Length: _____

Width: _____

Height: _____

Volume: _____

Object: Phone book

Length: _____

Width: _____

Height: _____

Volume: _____

Object: _____

Length: _____

Width: _____

Height: _____

Volume: _____

Object: _____

Length: _____

Width: _____

Height: _____

Volume: _____

Toss and Add

Take turns tossing five coins on the gameboard.
Read each number as your coin lands on it.
Keep a running total of your tosses.
Remember to line up the decimal points as you add.
The player with the highest score wins.

7.12	16.5	6.34	0.15
24.7	2.75	4.53	0.21
38.9	0.08	30.2	12.16
51.4	7.39	0.48	4.99

Shaping Up

Can you make these shapes? Outline and color each shape on the grid.

- yellow triangle
- brown right triangle
- blue square

- black rectangle
- purple parallelogram
- pink trapezoid

- orange pentagon
- green hexagon
- red octagon

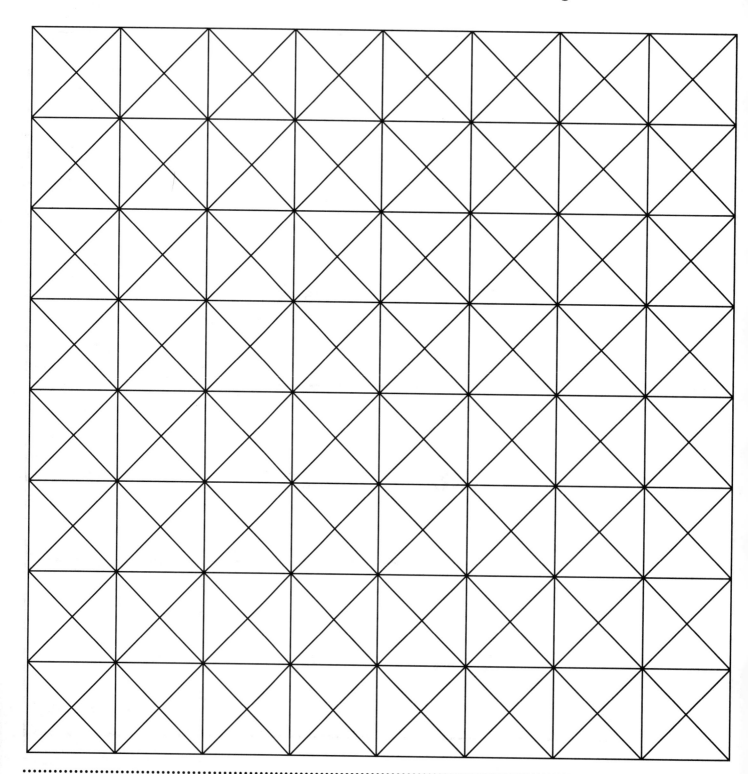

Weather or Not?

Keep a weather log for 5 days. Read, listen to, or watch the weather forecast. Record it on the chart along with the date. Then describe how the weather actually turned out. How accurate was the forecast?

Date	Forecaster and Weather Forecast	Actual Weather	Accuracy of Forecast

Settle Down!

Do this activity to discover what happens if you mix soil and water.

Materials:
a large jar with a lid, soil, water

Procedure:

1. Fill the jar about halfway with soil from the ground outside. Don't worry if the soil has rocks, sand, leaves, or other things mixed up in it. That makes it more interesting.

2. Add water to the jar so it's almost full. Put the lid on and shake it upside down for a minute. Draw how the jar looks. Predict how the jar will look in three hours. Draw your prediction.

3. Three hours later look carefully at the jar. Draw how it looks.

How the jar looks when first shook up	Prediction—How I think the jar will look	Results—How the jar looks 3 hours later

Finish these sentences.

I learned _____

_____

I think _____

_____

I wonder _____

_____

Healthful Eating

List everything you ate and drank yesterday.

Breakfast	Lunch	Dinner	Snacks

Study the food pyramid. Note how many servings a person should have each day from each food group. Then answer the questions.

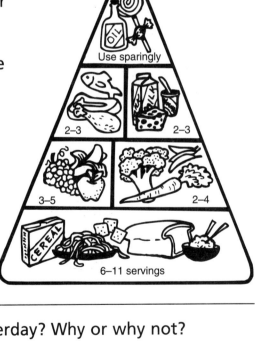

1. Did you eat more than, fewer than, or about the same number of suggested servings in each food group?

   bread, cereal, rice, pasta _____

   vegetables _____

   fruits _____

   milk, yogurt, cheese _____

   meat, poultry, fish,
   dry beans, eggs, nuts _____

2. Did you use fats, oils, and sweets sparingly? _____

3. Do you think you ate healthful meals and snacks yesterday? Why or why not?

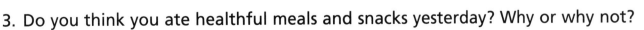

_____

_____

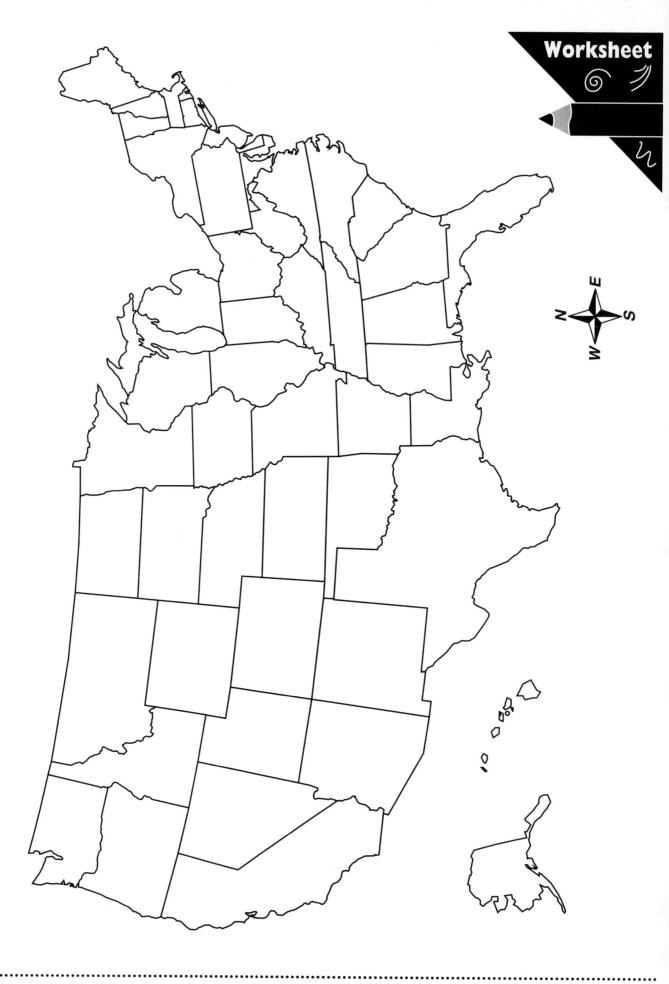

Show What You Know

Graph It!

Keep a record for one week of the hours and minutes you do homework, read for pleasure, listen to music, and watch TV. Calculate the total for each activity. Then round to the nearest hour.

	Mon.	Tues.	Wed.	Thurs.	Fri.	Sat.	Sun.	Total
Doing Homework								
Reading								
Listening to Music								
Watching TV								

Now record the information in this bar graph.

The Hours I Spent . . .

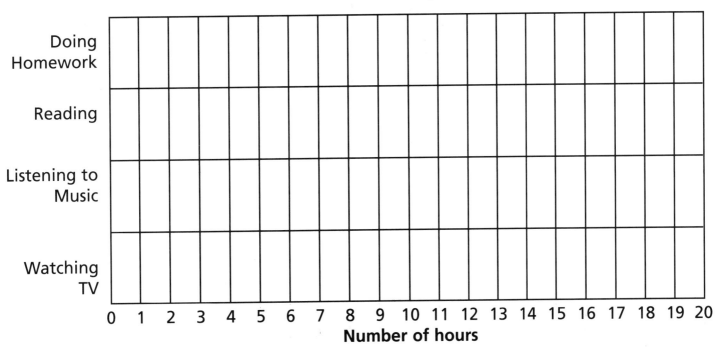

Presidential Facts

Do a little research to complete each statement about a president of the United States. Look in your social studies book, an encyclopedia, or children's almanacs. Then amaze your friends and family members with presidential facts.

☆ _____ was the first president to live in the White House.

☆ _____ was sworn into office on an airplane.

☆ _____ was the oldest person to be elected president.

☆ _____ and _____ both died on July 4, 1826.

☆ _____ was the only president to resign.

☆ _____ was the only president to serve two nonconsecutive terms (two terms not in a row).

☆ _____ was the first president to speak on the radio.

☆ _____ and _____ signed the Constitution.

☆ _____ was the first president to ride on a railroad train.

☆ _____ served the shortest time in office.

☆ _____ served the longest time in office.

☆ _____, the youngest person elected president, lived the shortest time.

☆ _____ was the only president who did not win election to the office of president or vice-president.

☆ _____ is the current president.

What a Plan!

1. List some things you would like to buy for yourself or your family.

_____

_____

_____

2. Look at your list. Which one do you want most? Make a check next to it. Then write why you want it so much.

_____

_____

3. Consider your choice. How much does it cost? Do you have enough money to buy it now? If not, how much more money do you need?

_____

_____

4. How can you get the money you need? Can you earn it and save it? Can you borrow the money and pay it back? List your ideas.

_____

_____

_____

5. Come up with a plan and write it below. Be sure to ask a parent for some suggestions.

_____

_____

_____

_____

6. Try out your plan. Good luck!

Word Menu

Keep a list of interesting food words. Write the word, the language it comes from, and what the word means.

Word	Origin	Meaning
sauerkraut	German	chopped cabbage, salted and fermented in its juices

Looking Around

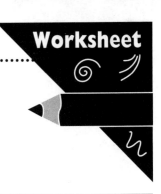

Go on an architectural search. Look for buildings in your community and other nearby communities that have these features, shapes, or materials. Tell where you saw each example and write a brief description of it. Add any other features, shapes, or materials you find to the chart.

Feature	Location	Description
column		
dome		
arch		

Shape	Location	Description
rectangle		
triangle		
semi-circle		

Material	Location	Description
brick		
wood		
stained glass		

Sound Syllables

This is the C scale. It shows the names of the notes and the sound syllables.

C	D	E	F	G	A	B	C	← Note names
do	re	mi	fa	so	la	ti	do	← Sound syllables

Write the note names and sound syllables for "Twinkle, Twinkle, Little Star." Sing the song first with the words and then with the sound syllables.

Twinkle, Twinkle, Little Star

Twin - kle, twin - kle, lit - tle star, how I won - der what you are.

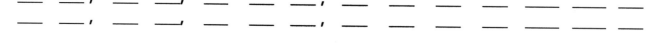

Up a - bove the world so high, like a dia - mond in the sky,

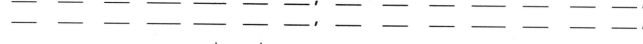

Twin - kle, twin - kle, lit - tle star, how I won - der what you are.

An Exercise Record

Keep an exercise record for one month.
Each day you exercise, write down what
you did and for how long.

Month _____

Sun.	Mon.	Tues.	Wed.	Thurs.	Fri.	Sat.

A Homework Contract

Child Section

I, _____, agree to do these
three items which relate to my homework:

1. _____

2. _____

3. _____

Positive consequences if I meet the terms of this contract:

Negative consequences if I do not meet the terms of this contract:

_____   _____
Signature   Date

Parent Section

I, _____, agree to do these
three items to support my child's homework activities:

1. _____

2. _____

3. _____

_____   _____
Signature   Date

 FS-23005 Skills for Success for Your Fourth Grader • © Frank Schaffer Publications, Inc.